Oven to Table Cooking

Oven to Table Cooking

Audrey Ellis

Illustrated by Kate Simunek

Hutchinson Benham

Oven temperature chart

Measurement notes

	deg. C	deg. F	Gas Mark
Very cool	110	225	$\frac{1}{4}$
	130	250	$\frac{1}{2}$
Cool	140	275	1
	150	300	2
Moderate	170	325	3
	180	350	4
Moderately hot	190	375	5
	200	400	6
Hot	220	425	7
	230	450	8
Very hot	240	475	9

All spoon measures given in the recipes are intended to be level.

Spoon measures are approximate and best used only for small quantities:

flour – 1 tablespoon = 15 g = $\frac{1}{2}$ oz

sugar – 1 tablespoon = 25 g = 1 oz

syrup, treacle, honey – 1 tablespoon = 25 g = 1 oz

breadcrumbs – 4 tablespoons = 25 g = 1 oz

8 tablespoons of liquid = 150 ml = $\frac{1}{4}$ pint

3 teaspoons = 1 tablespoon

Hutchinson Benham Limited
3 Fitzroy Square, London W1

An Imprint of the Hutchinson Group

London Melbourne Sydney Auckland
Wellington Johannesburg and agencies
throughout the world

First published 1977
© Text Denby Tableware Ltd 1977
© Illustrations Hutchinson Benham Ltd
1977

Set in Monophoto Imprint by
Photoprint Plates Ltd Rayleigh Essex

Printed in Great Britain by
The Anchor Press Ltd and bound by
Wm. Brendon & Son Ltd
both of Tiptree, Essex

ISBN 0 09 131570 0

Contents

Table linens supplied by Old Bleach
Furniture from the Denby Furniture Collection
Garden furniture from Bourne & Hollingsworth Ltd
Candles supplied by Prices Candles Ltd
Original photographic layout by Chris Sherratt
All photography by John Lee

Denby oven to tableware products featured in the colour plates

These tableware patterns are co-ordinated with Denby glass or crystal and cutlery selected from Denby Touchstone and Regency designs.

Note : In the U.S.A. the patterns marked * have different names:
Arabesque is known as 'Samarkand'
Rochester is known as 'Painters Pallette'

Introduction

Oven to table cooking is the most relaxing way, not only of entertaining, but also of coping with daily meal planning.

Most of the dishes in this book are cooked in the oven and, once ready, can be kept warm until your family gets home, or the late guest arrives. You, meanwhile, do not have to stand waiting for the right moment to start cooking the lamb chops, Steak Diane or Veal Cordon Bleu, as the case may be. There are exceptions of course, like soufflés, but these you need not commit to the oven until the guests are finishing their aperitifs, or the family is gathering around the table.

Let's start with casseroles

The rich blend of tempting flavours which results from combining everyday vegetables with meat and a few herbs and spices, produces a meal that pleases the senses of smell, sight and taste. Just the aroma that escapes as you lift the lid is a pleasure in itself, and stimulates the appetite. These are the dishes that can often be served without any accompaniment other than good crusty bread and a crisp salad on the side.

Casseroles are sometimes surprisingly economical because they make meat go a long way by balancing it with potatoes, pulses, pasta or rice: modestly priced ingredients most cooks have at hand in the kitchen. If the casserole is covered with a lid, one or two other dishes can be cooked at the same time in the oven, in a neighbourly fashion. Just take care that the aroma of curry does not add an unexpectedly exotic perfume to your chocolate rice pudding which may be in an open dish!

Casseroles are especially handy if you like to cook a quantity at one time, keeping some back for the next day. It is no old wives' tale that they taste better when reheated to serve again. The blending of flavours and intensity of the seasonings does seem to develop to a remarkable degree.

A newly married Victorian gentleman wrote to his mother: 'One cannot, as you say, expect marvels of a plain cook. I have taken your good advice, and ordered the beef stew to be served thin for servants' hall dinner on Tuesday, and in the dining room of a Wednesday. The improvement is astonishing.'

If you want to keep only part of a casserole for reheating, cover the surface of the food closely with foil or cling wrap, put on the lid and refrigerate the dish. Remove the close cover before reheating, and you will find the food has not dried out by contact with the air *inside* the empty part of the casserole.

The new watchword in cooking

Economy is a factor we would all prefer to forget about, but today it must be taken into account; otherwise the household budget soars and household accounts refuse to balance! For your family's sake you may be reluctant to save on buying the best quality food and cookware. But there is one side of catering where savings can be made without reducing the standard of your menus.

Oven heat is an expensive commodity, so make sure you exploit it to the full. Pack the oven with several items when it is in use – do not use it just for one lonely casserole. See the suggested menus for autotimed cooking (pages 114–118). These will give you the right idea about packing the oven properly, and using cooler areas for dishes that do not take kindly to high oven heat.

Some ovens are planned to give even heat throughout. However, this is no problem if you are at home to put in extra dishes and remove them at the right time; especially if you have the kind of cooker which has a smaller oven to which partially cooked dishes can be transferred. If this second oven is set to a very low heat, the dish will finish cooking with hardly any fuel cost. Sometimes the final stage is a flash of heat under the grill or broiler. Make sure the ovenproof dish will also withstand the fiercer heat. Stoneware will do so for any reasonable requirements.

Of course you rarely have to stay at home: most casserole dishes will bubble away contentedly in the safety of the oven while you go out shopping, drop in on a friend, or whatever you feel like doing. It hardly matters if you pause for a chat, or to have a cup of coffee, because the food will frequently tolerate another half hour of cooking time. On the other hand, casseroles are so good tempered that they rarely mind being cooked at a slightly higher heat to hurry them up if this is what you need.

What exactly is a casserole

By definition, a casserole is a flat-bottomed vessel with a closely fitting lid, and a handle or lugs. Some early casseroles would hardly have graced a dining table, but now that they are available in such beautiful shapes and patterns, it would be a pity to hide them away in the kitchen. Most of us claim (probably with justice) that we are not lazy about *necessary* dish washing, but no-one can deny the practicality as well as the joy of taking the cooked food from the oven straight to the table. You will certainly prefer to do this in a dish that is as pleasing to the eye as the contents are to the taste. If the pattern on the casserole co-ordinates with the tableware, so much the better.

Building up a good collection

Unless you are lucky enough to buy an extensive selection right away I suggest you begin your collection with those pieces which will serve the widest range of requirements. The obvious number one choice for most people would therefore be a large (approximately 2.2 litre/4 pint) casserole, since this can always be used for cooking smaller quantities. Later, you can add small and medium sized ones which are ideal for less than family sized meals which, if cooked in a large casserole, might have to include a disproportionate amount of liquid to cover the food properly These sizes are also ideal for cooking/serving vegetables – you can see how well this suits the baked potatoes served with Hungarian beef in red wine on page 35. Chapter one (on one pot family dinners) should give you plenty of ideas for imaginative casserole cooking, from the homely lamb's liver casserole to the party-piece Danish club streaky (illustrated on page 36).

Probably the second most useful single item is the shallow ovenproof dish, which travels from oven to table with even more ease than the casserole. As a cooking and serving piece it is unrivalled, for its shallowness displays well cooked and presented food to perfection. Saucy fish pie, illustrated on page 38, makes the point beautifully, as does in a different way chocolate and ginger date pudding (page

36), among many others. Another of its great virtues – one that you might not immediately think of – is its ability to double as a terrine. See page 93 where the buffet dish, layered terrine of chicken, is shown turned out from the oval dish in which it was cooked onto a matching serving platter.

Having got the nucleus of your ovenware collection, you can go on to acquire a huge range of more specialized items, such as soufflé dishes, covered soup bowls and ramekins, each ideally suited to its particular task. If you have chosen your range wisely to co-ordinate with your tableware, then there are many other pieces you are likely to want, such as soup bowls, salad bowls, and footed desserts. Another asset to bear in mind is that ovenproof dinner plates can be used when the occasion demands as pie plates. The delicious chestnut cheesecake photographed on page 94 was cooked in a flan ring on the plate and the ring then simply removed for serving.

Making your choice of ovenproof dishes

Many different materials are used to produce dishes for oven cookery. They must all withstand heat and staining. You can choose from enamelled cast iron or steel, ceramic or toughened glass, and many kinds of glazed pottery from earthenware to porcelain. A good choice in pottery is real stoneware which is durable, defies stains, is easy to clean and hygienic, and tough enough to withstand everyday use.

It is important to select real stoneware as there are many imitators of the stoneware style whose products do not have the same qualities in use.

Casseroles should not be chosen only for their good looks. Many of the rustic craft pottery dishes, for instance, are hand-thrown and will not balance well on an oven grid. There are also on the market some unglazed earthenware dishes which are porous and may even crack unless you go through the rigmarole of soaking them in cold water before cooking.

If you choose a range which has lugs rather than handles, they should be easy to hold, even wearing oven mitts or with a pan lifter, so that the dish will not slip from your grasp. If a handle is too long, you may have difficulty fitting it into the oven when other dishes have to be accommodated. The deep, narrow casserole (see illustration on page 36) is very suitable to place side by side with wider dishes.

The lid is a very important part of the whole dish and it must fit well. Rustic earthenware casseroles are often bad offenders in this respect. The lid should have a handle of a type which will let you remove it without burning your fingers. The type sunk in a dimple is almost impossible to grasp through several layers of protective cloth when hot. Removable handles need enormous care because it is possible to lock them in place incorrectly, and when you remove a full casserole from the oven the handle may suddenly part from it, subjecting you to a scalding hot shower of food. As a safety measure, always have a clear heatproof area or mat close to the oven door, so that if your grip on the casserole is not quite secure you can put it down quickly before an accident can occur.

Caring for your ovenproof dishes

You may find food crusted on the inner surface of your casseroles and gratin dishes (because that tends to happen when you cook in the oven). The best solution is to fill them to the brim and leave them soaking until they can literally be wiped clean. A gentle nylon scouring pad may be necessary, but a further soaking usually does the job equally well. The safest rule is to avoid scraping, and to rinse well in both water with detergent and then plain hot water.

Hints to make casserole cooking easier

GREASING A CASSEROLE This is inconvenient with the finger tips, or with a folded piece of wrapping paper. Put the fat on a small square of bread, use to grease evenly, then if appropriate you can break it apart and add it to the dish.

TIME SAVER: If the ingredients have all to be prepared, then mixed together in a bowl, do the mixing right in the greased casserole. That saves one dirty bowl you would otherwise have to wash.

FLAVOUR SAVER: Sometimes the quantity of food is just too large for one casserole, but only half-fills another. To keep the surface from drying out, cover with foil close to the food and mould up the inside as far as the rim, or even over the rim, so that you can use the lid to hold the foil in place. But foil is not cheap, so if you find yourself doing this very often, you would be better advised to add to your range by buying a small casserole.

GREAT ECONOMIZER: Leftover vegetables are often thrown away. If you intend using the oven for a casserole dish within the next 24 hours, put them in a covered dish in the refrigerator. When the oven is hot, put the vegetables with a knob of dripping or butter and a stock cube in another casserole, season to taste with paprika, curry powder or Worcestershire sauce and add 600 ml/1 pint/2½ cups boiling water. This makes a satisfying soup in less than an hour, and it can be slightly thickened towards the end with cornflour.

MAGICAL MARINADE: Meat which would be tough if roasted or grilled is often the best cut for casserole cooking. To tenderize it even more, marinate it for a few hours, or better still, overnight. Marinades are usually made of an acid ingredient (vinegar, lemon juice, leftover wine) and oil, seasoned in different ways with spices, herbs, garlic or onions. For white meats use white vinegar and wine; for red meats malt vinegar and red wine.

DRIED AND FRESH FRUIT: Just a hint of sweetness seems to do a lot to make casserole dishes tastier. No need to soak dried fruit, just add a few sultanas, raisins, dried apricots or prunes at the start. Fresh fruits such as apple, pear, pineapple and orange are also useful, but some may have to be added towards the end of cooking time, otherwise they disintegrate entirely. Lemon and orange juice, with the grated zest (the coloured outer part of the rind), improves many dishes.

FILLERS AND COVERS: An open casserole can be protected from drying out by a pastry lid, a topping of mashed or sliced raw potato and also less usual crusts, such as a scone topping, a crumble or diced fried bread. This is an alternative to simply covering with foil and makes the food go further. But where pasta and rice are included, not all recipes call for them to be cooked in the same dish with the other ingredients. Study the methods of cooking pasta, rice and even potatoes separately, but at the same time so that you can avoid cooking on top of the stove in a saucepan.

DECORATIVE GARNISHES: Some cooks complain that a casserole, when uncovered, could well be garnished, but do not see how. Finely chopped fresh herbs, especially parsley, mint and chives, contrast well with the colour of the food when scattered over the surface. Dumplings with fresh herbs add speckles of green, and caraway dumplings or a scone cobbler are decorative in themselves. Even a few frozen peas scattered over a cooked dish will cook sufficiently in steam if the lid is replaced for 2 minutes.

Co-ordinated table settings

No one who has eaten out in the last year or two can have failed to notice the rising cost of doing so. Luckily, the age of spiralling restaurant prices has coincided with – for most of us – a great improvement in housing standards so that more people than ever before have a home in which they can be proud to entertain. The trend is in any case towards a refreshing informality so that it is not necessary to struggle to reproduce the stiff atmosphere of white table-cloths and elaborate service, which so often in the past was used to disguise indifferent food and poor value for money. We have come a long way since the days when the kitchen was supposed to be separated from the dining room by a green baize door and several flights of stairs. Nowadays there may be no firm division between the two at all. There may be a see-through divider, or the dining-area may actually be a part of the kitchen. In either case it is important that you integrate the colour scheme carefully. The same old divisions that used to exist between kitchen utensils and dining room utensils have been swept away. Every cook knows what a delicate business it is to assemble a meal on serving dishes without letting anything get cool or spoiling the appearance of the food. The advent of oven-to-tableware makes the whole process simple and ensures that every dish will be served looking and tasting its very best. Incidentally, make sure your table mats are really heatproof; restoring a scorched table top to its pristine beauty is no joke.

The new informality gives you far more scope for your imagination, in the decoration and setting of your table as well as in the preparation of the food itself. You can set a scene that is pretty and charming or one that is dramatic. Naturally, the fact that there is no longer a safe conventional way of doing things means that the opportunity for disastrous errors has increased as much as the opportunity for stunning success. One way of making sure that you achieve the latter, not the former, is to choose a range of oven-to-tableware which also has matching or co-ordinating table settings. If you are setting up house for the first time, you have an ideal opportunity to make sure that everything you own harmonizes from the beginning. But even if you are not in that happy situation you can start with a few pieces and, if you choose the right range, you will know that the rest is available as and when you are in a position to add to your basic stock. Do not be tempted by something that looks attractive in the store or shop but does not relate to your colour schemes at home. You might be in for a big disappointment when you set out the pieces and find the colours clash with your curtains, or the prim flower pattern does not go with the vivid decor you have chosen for your room.

Visualize the effect in your own surroundings. If possible, buy one piece or arrange to take it on approval, and see how it looks in the proposed setting. When you are certain of your choice, look very carefully at the pieces available, and select those that fit in best with your life style and particularly your family style of eating. Are you sure to need cereal bowls? Must you have a matching coffee pot? Sometimes you end up wishing you had bought more soup coupes with covers or a salad bowl in the same pattern, which does double duty for sweets. Study the leaflets which show all the shapes before you actually order anything.

Table linen to match or contrast with your table can be greatly enhanced by napkins (either paper or linen) in plain colcurs, pale, delicate and fresh looking, or rich and deep for a touch of drama. Why not acquire the fascinating art of folding them in pretty shapes?

If you fumble over these, the simplest of all is to roll a napkin diagonally from one corner to the opposite one, then double the roll into a U-shape and press the bend down into wine or water goblets, so the two pointed ends stand up perkily. Linen napkins should be slightly stiffened with spray starch. For those who like to twist and fold something more elaborate, see the fold illustrated below.

If you feel this idea is too formal for your taste, just fold napkins in half and then diagonally, or in three, concertina fashion, and lay them on the side plates.

Co-ordination goes much further than planning a matched or contrasted arrangement of mats and napkins. If you choose a tablecloth, it should be easily laundered. Those which require careful washing and ironing tend to slip to the back of the linen shelves, and are seen no more! Fortunately many are now almost creaseproof and need little or no pressing. The daring can achieve remarkable results by piling pattern on pattern, some dainty, some bold, but all colour-related. You might decide on a patterned tablecloth with blending napkins of a different smaller pattern, and a flower arrangement with lots of small blooms, also related to the same basic colour.

For those who are not so bold, it is a good idea to choose, say, patterned stoneware to go with plain decor and accessories, or plain ware to go in a room with lots of eyecatching patterns. Too many, unless deftly handled, can war with each other and create a restless rather than a restful atmosphere.

Changes in Cutlery

One of the pleasantest surprises is finding that cutlery is available with handles to tone in with or match stoneware plates. These can really add warmth and colour to a table setting. It is a bonus if you can

Fold napkin in half and then in half again. Make accordian pleats from left to right. Press firmly. Open out and pull each indented area down one side (A). Open indentations on the other side (B). Press base together firmly and fan out top (C).

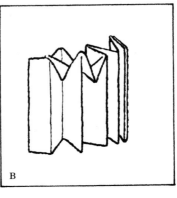
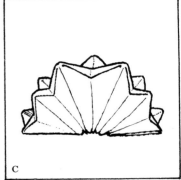

A   B   C

settle on coloured handles which go well with more than one range, although stainless steel or silver look well too. If the appointments are in natural wood (wooden handles to cutlery) follow through with wooden salad bowls, salt and pepper shakers and perhaps a round or oblong wooden dish as a base for candles or a flower arrangement. If all are in stainless steel, do not mingle them with some pieces in silver; they just do not seem planned to go together. Be creative with candles and flowers. Many containers not made for the purpose can be used as flower holders. If the shape is awkward, place a small, waterproof container inside. A flower-pinholder or ball of crumpled wire mesh prevents flowers from slipping or flopping about. Keep the arrangement low, as people find it irritating to peer at their friends through a screen of stems. Candle holders too are not really essential. You can set a candle firmly in a lump of plasticine in any chosen container. If you want to cover up the base with a posy of flowers, anchor one or two of the stems in the plasticine for extra firmness and pour a little water round the candle to keep the flowers fresh.

When garden flowers or wild ones are plentiful, gather them before the sun gets high and immediately place them in a bucket of water or inside a polythene bag in the shade; they will then last well. When fresh flowers are scarce and expensive, nothing is lovelier than an arrangement made with dried flowers and grasses. These are now dyed in subtle, contemporary colours, to suit every colour scheme. If you love tall candles, keep their shapes slim so they do not obscure the company from each other. Miniature ivy twisted round from the base almost up to the top can be secured invisibly by a short pin. By the way, candles do not shed tears of wax if placed in a freezer for 2–3 hours before being lit.

Wine and ways to serve it

In spite of the gradual rise in price, the consumption of wine everywhere has greatly increased, and many of us no longer regard it as something for special occasions only.

Fortunately many of the old embargoes on serving certain wines with certain dishes have disappeared. The general rules are few and simple.

1.   Dry, white and rosé wines now usually accompany fish, starters and white meats including poultry. Sweet white wines are served with desserts. Red wines are offered with red meat, dark meat of poultry, game and made-up dishes. Sometimes rosé is served throughout the meal.

2.   Dry white and rosé wines are chilled before opening the bottle and only uncorked at serving time. Red wines are uncorked and allowed to breathe and come up to room temperature before the meal starts. They are described as *chambré*, when the bottle is slightly warm to the touch. Don't try to hurry matters by putting the wine in front of the fire or plunging the bottles into very hot water. Especially for mature red wines of high quality, it is essential to stand the bottles upright at least one day beforehand to let any sediment settle. Fine mature red wines should be carefully decanted and stoppered to prevent loss of aroma and bouquet; less precious bottles left uncorked for two hours; robust young wines left uncorked anything from six to twelve hours. Sweet white wines may be served at room temperature.

3.   Any wine may be served in the round Paris goblet which holds 150ml/5 fluid ounces and is used in most restaurants. However, there are also special glasses for different wines. Those for white wine, drunk chilled, have long stems to grasp so that the warmth of your hand does not raise the temperature of the wine. Red wine is served in slightly larger glasses with a short stem, so it can be further warmed by clasping your hand round the bowl. Sparkling white wines, even champagne, are served in tall, narrow, tulip shaped glasses to preserve the sparkle as long as possible. Stoneware goblets may be warmed before pouring red wine into them, or chilled for white wine. Glasses, by contrast, do not retain their temperature long and do not affect the wine itself, although brandy glasses are sometimes warmed to release the aroma and flavour of the spirit quickly.

Even an undistinguished wine, correctly served, earns approval, and will taste better than if badly served. The order of serving, if you are offering more than one wine, is usually white wine before rosé, and then a bordeaux (claret) before the more robust burgundy. The second white wine which follows should be sweet.

When and how to use ice

Ice cubes or preferably crushed ice may be put into any mixed drink or cold punch, but not into glasses of table wine. You can simply crush ice cubes by wrapping them well in a cloth and shattering them with a hammer. For a big party bottles can be chilled in buckets. Half-fill a bucket with crushed ice and force the unopened bottles down into it so the surface of the ice reaches the necks. It is becoming usual to serve liqueurs as an apéritif, as well as with the coffee at the end of the meal. The usual measure of liqueur is poured into a larger glass half-filled with crushed ice.

How much wine to serve

It is usually reckoned that an average glass holds some 5 fluid ounces of wine. It is wise not to over-fill glasses as some space should be allowed to sample the bouquet before drinking. Standard bottles provide 5 generous glasses. The 1 litre/35 fl oz bottle serves 7 glasses. For a dinner party with sherry or other drinks beforehand allow for each person to have 2 or 3 glasses. Though the wine may be warm, the hostess must keep cool when a glass is overturned and red wine stains the table or cloth. Sprinkle the stain on a cloth at once with salt and get it off the table as soon as possible. Stretch the stained area over a bowl, sprinkle on more salt and pour boiling water through it, or warm water if the fabric is delicate. The table top should be mopped dry, wiped with a damp cloth sprinkled with a few drops of vinegar, dried and repolished. Luckily, white wine spills are not such a disaster.

Here are two recipes, one for a hot red wine punch and the other for a chilled white wine punch.

Pickwick punch: Place 4 cloves, 1 small cinnamon stick and 4 tablespoons soft (light) brown sugar in a jug. Add 100 ml/ 4 fl oz/½ cup boiling water. Cover and allow to infuse for about 25 minutes, until cold. Strain into a large saucepan, discarding the flavourings. Add 2 tablespoons brandy and 1 litre/1¾ pints/scant 5 cups robust red wine. Heat to just below boiling point then transfer to a warmed stoneware

jug and serve in stoneware wine cups, each topped with a slice of lemon. *Serves 4–6.*

Primrose pathfinder: Pour one 2 litre/2½ pints/6¼ cups bottle dry white wine into a large punch bowl. Add 3 measures of gin, 1 measure of lemon juice and 1 large bottle fizzy lemonade or other sweet carbonated water. Just before serving add a few cubes of ice and float lemon slices on top. (If a sweeter punch is preferred, use sweet white wine.) *Serves 8.*

How to store wine

Wine racks are reasonable in price and offer by far the best home for your wine. Put the rack in a cool place out of direct light. The bottles are stored horizontally to prevent the corks from drying out. It is a problem to decide whether to open a bottle of table wine too long in advance, to use some for cooking. The best solution is to store *leftovers* of wine and use these up instead. White wine, transferred to a small bottle which leaves little air space between the wine surface and the cork, keeps well in the refrigerator for up to a week. Red wine, with a spoonful of sherry or brandy added, keeps for two weeks – but only to be used for cooking of course. Both varieties can be stored for months in the freezer in polythene tumblers with a seal. Leave one-tenth of the volume of the container empty for expansion in freezing. (It is a comparatively new idea to buy wine in plastic sachets for cooking.)

How to set the glasses or goblets

A table setting for one person at which white and red wines are to be served is shown on page 17 (see photograph at top right). The menu includes a cold soup, a main dish of meat, and a pudding (rather than a cold dessert).

The touches that count

Extra care in making the table look attractive is worth while, even just for the family, but more so for guests. Little nibbles are much appreciated with drinks before the meal; if only because many people find alcohol hard to take on an empty stomach, and of course they are paying you the compliment of coming hungry to the table.

NIBBLES: Scraps of puff paste make very welcoming titbits. Roll them out, spread with a savoury meat or yeast extract, sprinkle with chopped nuts and bake them off. Or, if you have more pastry to spare, roll it out thinly to a square shape, sprinkle with rock salt, pepper and grated cheese, and roll inwards from two opposite sides to the middle. Seal with egg, cut off slices, and bake in a hot oven for about 15 minutes. (Remember, always use a hot oven for puff pastry.) They look like the sweet *palmier* biscuits and are delicious.

ROLLS: Warm rolls are much nicer than cold ones. Sprinkle the tops with a little cold water and pop them in a moderately hot oven to heat and get crisp.

BUTTER: There is no need to put butter on the table in a solid block, which people find hard to cut. Warm the knife in hot water, then slice the butter vertically end to end, in strips as wide as your finger tip. Slice again, the same distance apart, crossways. You will then have plenty of nice little oblong pats to pile up on a butter dish. If you invest in a pair of wooden butter pats, you can make prettily marked butter balls. The trick is to keep dipping the pats into iced water and turn the oblong of butter each time you bang it between the butter pats to produce a criss-cross pattern.

LEMONS: Lemons are easy to transform into very decorative garnishes. Begin with wedges, by cutting the lemon in half lengthways from the stem to the opposite end. Cut each half into four, also lengthways, trim any surface membrane or pith. Then experiment with lemons cut in half crossways. Cut a sliver from the peel each end, so the halves will sit firmly on a plate, cut side up. Peel a thin section of rind from the cut edge all the way round, but not quite meeting, so that the section remains attached to the lemon half. Take the end and tie a single knot, resting close to the flesh, with the loose end turning up. The lemon halves can be squeezed, but look almost too pretty to be used for this practical purpose. (See drawing on page 19.)

MELON BOATS: What about serving a wedge of melon as a starter, in a more decorative form than usual? Begin by removing the seeds from the wedge, then slice it away from the rind, using a curved grapefruit knife, if you have one, but do not remove it. Run a straight knife down the centre from one end to the other, cutting through to the rind. Now cut slices across the width of your thumb, without removing them. Push slices out alternately to each side, to make a turret effect. It is then very easy to eat the melon with a fork. (See drawing on page 19.)

Four co-ordinated table settings.

 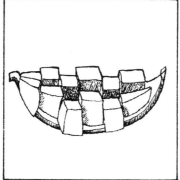 

Lemon knots   *Melon boats*   *Pineapple bows*

PINEAPPLE BOWS: For a more compli-cated variation with a pineapple wedge, take a quarter of a small pineapple, cut from the leafy end downwards, and cut the flesh away from the hard skin with a grape-fruit knife, without removing it. Then cut down with a straight knife inside the quarter-core running down the centre, and you will have loosened an inner section the shape of an apple slice. Cut it through like the melon in slices the width of your thumb, then push each section out alter-nately in opposite directions. (See draw-ing above.)

FINGER BOWLS: As a final touch, if any of the food needs handling which is messy, provide guests with small bowls of water, with a squeeze of lemon juice in it, and float a few flower petals on the surface of each to indicate that they are finger bowls, and not for drinking!

Two party punches: the cold primrose pathfinder and, to its right, hot Pickwick punch. In the foreground, a selection of cheesy savouries.

Chapter 1
One pot family dinners

The challenging task of cooking at least one main meal every day for a hungry family becomes formidable if you run out of time and ideas. Comments from your nearest and dearest are liable to be frank. 'Must we have sausages every Wednesday? . . . Is there only one recipe in the world for stew? . . . Must we have that meat pie *again*?' Wounding, if true or not, but there is an easy way out.

Build up a repertoire of really delicious one-pot dinners, which will allow you to change the menu daily for weeks on end, and vary it considerably from one season to another. For health's sake, you may decide to make up a green salad, really fresh and crisp; or cook a green vegetable for just a few minutes in very little water, as well. These are last-minute decisions to be taken at the time you decide to lay the table. But the heart of the satisfying meal can be a dish that cooks itself without attention in the oven, and fills each plate to please everyone. From a nutritional viewpoint, the salad or extra vegetable can be dispensed with if you serve a big bowl of fresh fruit instead of a cooked pudding.

The savings are considerable, when you come to think about it. There is a great saving in your *time*, because once the preparation is completed (and this can often be done earlier in the day) the minutes you need to spend in the kitchen during the hour before the meal are limited. What a boon this is when children and adults are arriving home, the phone and door bell never seem to stop ringing, and it is often just that hour which is the

busiest one of the day. If you cook king-size quantities, and freeze future meals, the saving is even greater.

There is a great saving in *cost*, because most one-pot dinners utilize cheap cuts, or at least rarely the expensive grilling and roasting cuts. Then there is the saving in cost because only one source of heat need be used. The oven is so accommodating: rolls can be popped in to warm up, made-up dishes to reheat, and a sweet dish which needs to cook and cool down for the following day. My baked egg custards are always made like this, and I never need heat the oven specially for them, unless I want to serve them hot.

There is a great saving in *effort* because food goes straight to the table in the cooking vessel. No time is wasted dishing up, or washing up endless pans. Even your increased confidence that the meal cannot be spoiled by bad timing, or can be 'stretched' in so many ways to feed a casual guest, saves anxiety, a form of frittering away our energy; which with some housewives involves more actual effort than the preparation of a meal. Five pork chops will not divide up easily to feed six people. These subdivisions are much easier when food is cooked by the one-pot method.

Confidence in receiving compliments on your cooking, or just the occasional remark that you are a marvellous cook, brings you many rewards. Pride in doing something well, but not wastefully, for a start. Plus undiminished enthusiasm to tackle the job of catering for a family every day of the year.

Cod and potato casserole ✳

METRIC/IMPERIAL	AMERICAN
2 large potatoes	2 large potatoes
4 thick cod steaks	4 thick cod steaks
40 g/1½ oz butter	3 tablespoons butter
1 tablespoon flour	1 tablespoon flour
1 small onion, grated	1 small onion, grated
396 g/14 oz can tomatoes, sieved	14 oz can tomatoes, sieved
salt and mild paprika pepper to taste	salt and mild paprika pepper to taste
1 teaspoon dried dill weed	1 teaspoon dried dill weed

Thinly slice the potatoes and soak in cold water to cover. Place the cod steaks in a buttered shallow ovenproof dish and bake uncovered in a moderate oven (180°C, 350°F, Gas Mark 4) for 5 minutes. Melt half the butter in a saucepan, stir in the flour and grated onion. Gradually add the sieved tomatoes and their liquid, and salt and paprika pepper. Bring to the boil, stirring constantly, then pour over the fish. Drain the potato slices and arrange in a thin layer, overlapping, over the fish. Dot with the remaining butter and sprinkle lightly with paprika. Cover and return to the oven for 30 minutes. The potatoes will turn almost orange in colour. Serve sprinkled with the dill.   *Serves 4.* If frozen, reheat and sprinkle with dill at serving time.

Super fish pie ✳

METRIC/IMPERIAL	AMERICAN
350 g/12 oz cod fillet	¾ lb cod fillet
150 ml/¼ pint milk	¾ cup milk
150 ml/¼ pint water	½ cup water
25 g/1 oz butter	2 tablespoons butter
25 g/1 oz plain flour	¼ cup flour
1 tablespoon lemon juice	1 tablespoon lemon juice
1 tablespoon chopped parsley	1 tablespoon chopped parsley
1 hard-boiled egg, chopped	1 hard-boiled egg, chopped
50 g/2 oz stuffed green olives, sliced	¼ cup sliced stuffed green olives
225 g/8 oz puff pastry	½ lb basic puff pastry
little beaten egg	little beaten egg

Put the fish fillet into a pan with the milk and water. Cover and poach for 10 minutes. Lift the fish from the pan with a slotted draining spoon and reserve the liquid. Remove skin and bones and flake the fish. Melt the butter in a clean saucepan and stir in the flour. Cook for 2 minutes, gradually add the strained fish liquid and bring to the boil, stirring constantly. Add the lemon juice, parsley and chopped hard-boiled egg, season to taste and fold in the flaked fish. Cool and add the olives. Roll out the pastry to a 30 cm/12 in square. Trim the edges. Put the fish mixture in the centre of the pastry, fold up the corners like an envelope, damp the edges and seal well. Place on a damped oven-proof plate. Brush with beaten egg and bake in a moderately hot oven (200°C, 400°F, Gas Mark 6) for 30 minutes, until well risen and golden.   *Serves 4.* If frozen, reheat.

Casserole of tuna with tomatoes ✳

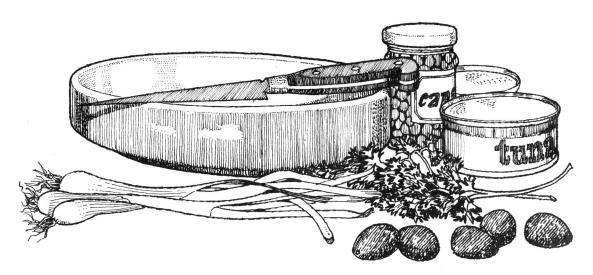

METRIC/IMPERIAL
1 tablespoon oil
2 198 g/7 oz cans tuna
3 spring onions, chopped
2 tablespoons chopped parsley
2 canned red pimentoes, chopped
8 cooked new potatoes, diced
8 black olives, stoned
250 ml/8 fl oz tomato juice
salt and pepper to taste
1 tablespoon drained capers

AMERICAN
1 tablespoon oil
2 7 oz cans tuna
3 scallions, chopped
2 tablespoons chopped parsley
2 canned red pimentoes, chopped
8 cooked small potatoes, diced
8 black olives, pitted
1 cup tomato juice
salt and pepper to taste
1 tablespoon drained capers

Pour the oil into a shallow ovenproof dish. Turn the contents of the cans of tuna into a basin and roughly flake the fish. Add the chopped onions, parsley, pimento, potato and olives. Spoon into the casserole, pour over the tomato juice and season to taste. Sprinkle over the capers and cook in a moderate oven (180°C, 350°F, Gas Mark 4) for 30–35 minutes. *Serves 4.*

✳ This symbol indicates recipe suitable for freezing.

Saucy fish pie ✳ *(Illustrated on page 38)*

METRIC/IMPERIAL	AMERICAN
450 g/1 lb white fish fillet	*1 lb white fish fillet*
600 ml/1 pint milk	*2½ cups milk*
50 g/2 oz butter	*¼ cup butter*
1 large onion, chopped	*1 large onion, chopped*
25 g/1 oz flour	*¼ cup flour*
½ teaspoon Worcestershire sauce	*½ teaspoon Worcestershire sauce*
100 g/4 oz Cheddar cheese, grated	*1 cup grated Cheddar cheese*
450 g/1 lb hot boiled potatoes	*1 lb hot boiled potatoes*
1 egg, beaten, and a little milk	*1 egg, beaten, and a little milk*

Cut the fish into bite-sized pieces and place in a saucepan. Season and pour over the milk. Poach gently for about 10 minutes, until the fish flakes easily with a fork. Strain off the milk and reserve. Melt the butter in a clean saucepan and use to fry the onion gently until soft. Stir in the flour then gradually add the strained milk and bring to the boil, stirring constantly. Cook for 2 minutes then add the Worcestershire sauce and most of the cheese and stir until the cheese has melted. Carefully fold in the cooked fish and season to taste with salt and pepper. Transfer the mixture to a greased ovenproof pie dish. Mash the hot potatoes and beat in the egg and sufficient milk to give a creamy texture. Place in a piping bag fitted with a star nozzle and pipe the potato decoratively around the top of the fish mixture. Garnish with sliced tomato if wished. Sprinkle the uncovered surface of the fish mixture with the remaining cheese and bake in a moderate oven (180°C, 350°F, Gas Mark 4) for 25–30 minutes, until the potato topping is crisp and golden brown.   *Serves 4*. If frozen sprinkle with extra cheese before reheating.

Veal and apricot curry ✳

METRIC/IMPERIAL	AMERICAN
75 g/3 oz butter	*⅓ cup butter*
1 tablespoon oil	*1 tablespoon oil*
¾ kg/1½ lb veal, diced	*1½ lb veal, diced*
1 medium onion, chopped	*1 medium onion, chopped*
1 tablespoon curry powder	*1 tablespoon curry powder*
1 clove garlic, crushed	*1 clove garlic, crushed*
100 g/4 oz dried apricots, chopped	*¾ cup chopped dried apricots*
225 g/8 oz long grain rice	*generous 1 cup long grain rice*
50 g/2 oz seedless raisins	*¼ cup seedless raisins*
50 g/2 oz salted peanuts	*¼ cup salted peanuts*
½ teaspoon ground ginger	*½ teaspoon ground ginger*
700 ml/1¼ pints chicken stock	*3 cups chicken broth*

Heat the butter and oil in a saucepan and use to brown the veal on all sides. Add the onion, curry powder, garlic, apricots and rice and cook for 5 minutes, stirring. Transfer to a medium ovenproof casserole and add the raisins, peanuts, ginger and chicken stock. Season to taste with salt and a little pepper if necessary. Cover and cook in a moderate oven (180°C, 350°F, Gas Mark 4) for 45–55 minutes, or until tender.   *Serves 4*. If frozen, reheat.

Worcester beef with dumplings ✳

METRIC/IMPERIAL
1 large onion
1 large parsnip
1 tablespoon oil
450 g/1 lb minced beef
1 beef stock cube
300 ml/½ pint water
1 tablespoon Worcestershire sauce
salt and pepper to taste
100 g/4 oz flour
¼ teaspoon salt
50 g/2 oz shredded suet
1 tablespoon chopped parsley
water to mix

AMERICAN
1 large onion
1 large parsnip
1 tablespoon oil
1 lb ground beef
1 beef bouillon cube
1¼ cups water
1 tablespoon Worcestershire sauce
salt and pepper to taste
1 cup flour
¼ teaspoon salt
½ cup shredded suet
1 tablespoon chopped parsley
water to mix

Chop the onion and parsnip. Heat the oil in a saucepan, add the minced beef, onion and parsnip, and cook gently until the meat is lightly browned. Dissolve the stock cube in the water and add to the meat with the Worcestershire sauce. Season to taste with salt and pepper. When just boiling, pour into a large ovenproof casserole. Cover and cook in a moderate oven (180°C, 350°F, Gas Mark 4) for 15 minutes. To make the dumplings, sift the flour and salt into a basin. Add the shredded suet and chopped parsley. Add sufficient water to make a fairly stiff dough. Turn onto a floured surface, divide into 8 pieces and shape each piece into a ball. Remove the casserole from the oven and arrange the dumplings on top. Return to the oven and cook for a further 20 minutes. If you like soft spongy dumplings, cook with the lid on the casserole. If you prefer a crisper finish, cook uncovered. *Serves 4.* If frozen, pack dumplings boiled in water separately, add before reheating.

Rich Spanish stew ✳

METRIC/IMPERIAL	AMERICAN
¾ kg/1½ lb stewing beef	1½ lb stewing beef
2 leeks	2 leeks
2 tablespoons oil	2 tablespoons oil
1 clove of garlic, crushed	1 clove of garlic, crushed
3 carrots, 1 stick celery, sliced	3 carrots, 1 stalk celery, sliced
15 g/½ oz flour	1 tablespoon flour
450 ml/¾ pint beef stock	2 cups beef stock
396 g/14 oz can tomatoes	14 oz can tomatoes
1 bay leaf	1 bay leaf
4 stuffed green olives, sliced	4 stuffed green olives, sliced

Cut meat into cubes, trim and finely slice the leeks. Rinse thoroughly and drain. Fry the beef in the oil until browned all over. Drain and remove from the pan. Add the garlic and prepared vegetables to the oil in the pan and fry gently for 5 minutes. Stir in the flour, and cook gently for about 10 minutes until golden brown. Stir in the stock, tomatoes and their liquid. Add the bay leaf and season to taste. Place the meat, vegetables and sauce in a large ovenproof casserole and cook in a cool oven (150°C, 300°F, Gas Mark 2) for 2½–3 hours, until the meat is very tender. Remove the bay leaf and stir in the olives. Serve with plain oven-baked rice. (See page 61 for method).   *Serves 4.* If frozen, add olives before reheating.

Beef casserole with oatmeal crunchies ✳

METRIC/IMPERIAL	AMERICAN
1 kg/2 lb chuck steak	2 lb chuck steak
25 g/1 oz dripping	2 tablespoons dripping
4 medium onions, chopped	4 medium onions, chopped
3 tablespoons tomato purée	3 tablespoons tomato paste
300 ml/½ pint red wine	1¼ cups red wine
½ teaspoon sugar	½ teaspoon sugar

topping:

225 g/8 oz self raising flour, 100 g/4 oz medium oatmeal, large pinch of salt, 175 g/6 oz butter, little milk	2 cups all-purpose flour sifted with 2 teaspoons baking powder, 1 cup old-fashioned oats, large dash of salt, ¾ cup butter, little milk

Trim the meat and cut into bite-sized pieces. Melt the fat and use to brown the meat. Add the onion and fry gently for about 2 minutes. Stir in the tomato purée, wine, sugar and season to taste. Transfer to a medium ovenproof casserole, cover and cook in a moderate oven (180°C, 350°F, Gas Mark 4) for 1½ hours. Mix together the flour, oatmeal and salt. Rub in the butter and add sufficient water to make a stiff dough. Divide into 12 equal portions and roll each into a ball. Flatten the balls gently with floured hands and arrange on top of the meat mixture. Brush with milk and return to the oven, uncovered, for a further 30 minutes.   *Serves 6.* If frozen, reheat.

Braised beef in red wine ✳

METRIC/IMPERIAL
¾–1 kg/1½–2 lb braising steak, in
  one piece
salt and pepper to taste
2 tablespoons oil
2 carrots
2 small turnips
2 small parsnips
1 large onion
2 tomatoes
150 ml/¼ pint robust red wine
2 teaspoons cornflour
6 large potatoes

AMERICAN
1½–2 lb chuck or blade steak, in one
  piece
salt and pepper to taste
2 tablespoons oil
2 carrots
2 small turnips
2 small parsnips
1 large onion
2 tomatoes
½ cup robust red wine
2 teaspoons cornstarch
6 large potatoes

Sprinkle the meat all over with salt and pepper then brush all over with oil. Place in a covered casserole for 24 hours to tenderize it. Dice the root vegetables and quarter the tomatoes. Put the prepared vegetables into a large ovenproof casserole, and then lay the joint on top. Pour over the wine, cover and place on a baking sheet. Scrub the potatoes, prick the skin in several places, brush with oil and place round the casserole on the baking sheet. Cook in a moderate oven (180°C, 350°F, Gas Mark 4) for 2½ hours. Moisten the cornflour with a little water. Remove the casserole lid and stir the cornflour mixture into the braise. Raise the oven to heat to moderately hot (200°C, 400°F, Gas Mark 6) and remove the potatoes from the baking sheet. Return the braise, uncovered, to the oven for a further 10 minutes to brown the meat.   *Serves 6*. If frozen, boil potatoes separately while reheating.

Variations:

Hungarian beef with red wine
(Illustrated on page 35)

Before placing the casserole in the oven add 4 tablespoons soured cream, 2 chopped anchovy fillets, 1 tablespoon lemon juice, grated zest (rind) of 1 lemon, 1 tablespoon drained capers, 1 crushed clove of garlic and a dash of hot paprika pepper to the braise.

French beef

Marinate the meat as in the basic recipe, then brown in 2 tablespoons of oil, place in the casserole, add six whole onions, 1 bay leaf and a pinch (dash) of dried thyme. Pour over 150 ml/¼ pint/½ cup white wine. Before serving sprinkle with chopped parsley.

Piquant beef

Three hours before braising make 2 deep slits lengthwise in the joint and coat the inside of the slits thickly with 2 tablespoons prepared mild mustard.

Beef casserole with * corn dumplings

METRIC/IMPERIAL	AMERICAN
1 small green pepper	*1 small green pepper*
2 tablespoons oil	*2 tablespoons oil*
2 large onions, sliced	*2 large onions, sliced*
2 large carrots, sliced	*2 large carrots, sliced*
¾ kg/1½ lb lean chuck steak, cubed	*1½ lb lean chuck steak, cubed*
2 tablespoons flour	*2 tablespoons flour*
396 g/14 oz can tomatoes	*14 oz can tomatoes*
2 tablespoons tomato purée	*2 tablespoons tomato paste*
2 beef stock cubes	*2 beef bouillon cubes*
450 ml/¾ pint boiling water	*2 cups boiling water*

topping:

100 g/4 oz self raising flour	*1 cup all-purpose flour, sifted with*
	1 teaspoon baking powder
50 g/2 oz shredded suet	*½ cup shredded suet*
175 g/7 oz can sweetcorn kernels	*1¼ cups kernel corn*
6 tablespoons cold water	*6 tablespoons cold water*

Deseed and slice the green pepper. Heat the oil in a large saucepan. Add the sliced onions, carrots, and green pepper and fry gently for 5 minutes. Remove the vegetables from the pan. Add the meat and fry until golden brown on all sides. Return the onions, carrots, and green pepper to the pan. Sprinkle over the flour, and stir into the meat. Add the tomatoes with their liquid, and the tomato purée. Dissolve the stock cubes in the boiling water, and stir into the meat mixture, with seasoning to taste. Transfer to a medium ovenproof casserole. Cover and cook in a moderate oven (180°C, 350°F, Gas Mark 4) for 2 hours. Meanwhile, mix the flour with the suet, and a good pinch of salt. Add two heaped tablespoons of sweetcorn, and mix to a fairly soft dough with the cold water. Divide the dumpling mixture into eight portions, and shape each one into a ball. Remove the casserole from the oven, and stir in the remaining corn. Arrange the dumplings on top. Return to the oven and cook, uncovered, for a further 25 minutes, until the dumplings are well risen and cooked. *Serves 4.* If frozen, make dumplings, add corn to casserole and cook dumplings while it reheats after defrosting.

Lamb pie with pears ✱
(Illustrated on page 38)

METRIC/IMPERIAL
450 g/1 lb boneless shoulder lamb, cubed
2 medium onions, sliced
salt and pepper to taste
1 teaspoon dried marjoram
¾ teaspoon ground ginger
150 ml/¼ pint beef stock
1 tablespoon cornflour
225 g/8 oz puff pastry
3 medium pears
150 ml/¼ pint soured cream
1 egg, beaten

AMERICAN
1 lb boneless shoulder of lamb, cubed
2 medium onions, sliced
salt and pepper to taste
1 teaspoon dried marjoram
¾ teaspoon ground ginger
½ cup beef broth
1 tablespoon cornstarch
½ lb puff paste
3 medium pears
½ cup soured cream
1 egg, beaten

Fry lamb cubes without extra fat until brown. Add the onion and fry for a further 10 minutes. Add the seasoning, herbs, ginger and stock. Cover and simmer for 1 hour. Moisten the cornflour with a little cold water, stir into the pan and bring to the boil, stirring constantly. Cook for 2 minutes and allow to cool. Roll out the pastry thinly to a large square and sprinkle lightly with more ginger. Spoon the meat mixture into the centre of the pastry. Peel, core and slice the pears and place on the meat mixture. Top with the soured cream. Fold up the corners of the pastry to overlap in the centre and produce an envelope shape. Brush the edges with beaten egg and seal well together. Place in a shallow ovenproof dish, brush all over with beaten egg and bake in a hot oven (220°C, 425°F, Gas Mark 7) for 25–30 minutes until golden brown.   *Serves 4.*

Stroganoff casserole

METRIC/IMPERIAL
2 breasts of lamb, boned
2 large onions, sliced
2 teaspoons dried rosemary
25 g/1 oz flour
salt and pepper to taste
450 ml/¾ pint beef stock
2 large potatoes
150 ml/¼ pint natural yogurt

AMERICAN
2 breasts of lamb, boned
2 large onions, sliced
2 teaspoons dried rosemary
¼ cup flour
salt and pepper to taste
2 cups beef broth
2 large potatoes
½ cup plain yogurt

Trim the breasts and cut the meat into narrow strips. Fry them in their own fat until crisp and golden brown. Drain, and place in a medium ovenproof casserole. Add the onions to the fat in the pan and fry until soft. Stir in the rosemary, flour and seasoning. Gradually add the stock, and bring to the boil, stirring constantly. Pour over the meat. Thinly slice the potatoes, and arrange overlapping on the meat. Pour over the yoghurt and cook in a moderate oven (180°C, 350°F, Gas Mark 4) for 1½ hours.   *Serves 4.*

Curried neck of lamb ✱

METRIC/IMPERIAL	AMERICAN
1 cooking apple	*1 baking apple*
¾ kg/1½ lb potatoes, sliced	*1½ lb potatoes, sliced*
4 medium onions, sliced	*4 medium onions, sliced*
8 best end of neck of lamb chops	*8 rib of lamb chops*
1 small bay leaf	*1 small bay leaf*
2 sprigs rosemary	*2 sprigs rosemary*
1 teaspoon tomato purée	*1 teaspoon tomato paste*
1 tablespoon curry powder	*1 tablespoon curry powder*
600 ml/1 pint beef stock	*2½ cups beef broth*

Peel, core and slice the apple and layer in an ovenproof casserole with the potato, onion, chops, and herbs. Stir the tomato purée and curry powder into the stock. Pour over the meat and vegetables. Cover and cook in a moderate oven (180°C, 350°F, Gas Mark 4) for 1 hour or until the meat is tender. Remove the lid, taste and add salt if necessary. Return to the oven, uncovered, for a further 20 minutes to brown the top.   *Serves 4.* If frozen, cook uncovered only while reheating.

Kiwi cook-in ✱

METRIC/IMPERIAL	AMERICAN
1 kg/2 lb neck of lamb chops	*2 lb neck of lamb slices*
2 large onions, sliced	*2 large onions, sliced*
225 g/8 oz swede, diced	*½ lb rutabaga, diced*
225 g/8 oz turnip, diced	*½ lb turnip, diced*
25 g/1 oz flour	*¼ cup flour*
1 teaspoon dried mixed herbs	*1 teaspoon dried mixed herbs*
600 ml/1 pint beef stock	*2½ cups beef broth*
salt and pepper to taste	*salt and pepper to taste*
220 g/7¾ oz can baked beans	*1 cup baked beans*

Fry the chops gently in their own fat for 5 minutes on each side. Drain, and place in a large ovenproof casserole. Add the onions, swede and turnip to the fat remaining in the pan, and fry until soft. Stir in the flour and herbs. Gradually add the stock and bring to the boil, stirring constantly; season to taste. Pour over the meat and cook in a moderate oven (180°C, 350°F, Gas Mark 4) for 1½ hours. Add the baked beans, stir well, and return to the oven for a further 30 minutes.   *Serves 4–5.* If frozen, reheat.

Tipsy lamb casserole ✳

METRIC/IMPERIAL
1 tablespoon oil
¾–1 kg/1½–2 lb middle neck of lamb chops
450 g/1 lb potatoes, sliced
salt and pepper to taste
1 large onion, sliced
450 g/1lb cooking apples, sliced
1 beef stock cube
450 ml/¾ pint dry cider
1 tablespoon vermouth
chopped mint

AMERICAN
1 tablespoon oil
1½–2 lb neck of lamb slices
1 lb potatoes, sliced
salt and pepper to taste
1 large onion, sliced
1 lb baking apples, sliced
1 beef bouillon cube
1½ cups cider
2 tablespoons vermouth
chopped mint

Heat the oil in a pan, add the chops and fry until brown on both sides. Cover the sliced potato with cold water. Add ½ teaspoon salt and bring to boiling point. Drain off the liquid, reserve and arrange half the potato in the bottom of a large ovenproof casserole. Put the meat, onion and sliced apple in a layer on top and finish with the remaining potato. Brush over with a little oil. Dissolve the stock cube in the cider and vermouth and pour into the casserole. Cook in a moderately hot oven (190°C, 375°F, Gas Mark 5) for 1½–2 hours, until the meat is tender and the potatoes cooked: Serve garnished with a little chopped mint.   *Serves 4–6*. If frozen, reheat and garnish at serving time.

Sherried chicken Cadiz ✳

METRIC/IMPERIAL
25 g/1 oz butter
1 tablespoon oil
4 chicken portions
100 g/4 oz piece streaky bacon
12 button onions
25 g/1 oz flour
150 ml/¼ pint sherry
150 ml/¼ pint chicken stock
salt and pepper to taste
12 stuffed green olives
chopped parsley

AMERICAN
2 tablespoons butter
1 tablespoon oil
4 chicken portions
¼ lb piece bacon
12 baby onions
¼ cup flour
½ cup sherry
¾ cup chicken broth
salt and pepper to taste
12 stuffed green olives
chopped parsley

Melt the butter and oil in a frying pan and fry the chicken portions until golden brown all over. Remove and place in a large ovenproof casserole. Cut the bacon into strips and add to the fat remaining in the pan with the onions. Fry until the bacon is golden brown. Stir in the flour and cook for 2 minutes. Add the sherry and stock and bring to the boil, stirring constantly, until thickened. Season to taste. Pour the sauce over the chicken, cover and cook in a moderately hot oven (180°C, 350°F, Gas Mark 4) for about 1 hour or until the chicken is tender. Add the olives and serve sprinkled with parsley and accompanied by fresh crusty bread.   *Serves 4*. If frozen reheat and add olives and parsley when serving.

Country chicken pie ✳
(illustrated on page 38)

METRIC/IMPERIAL
50 g/2 oz quick cook macaroni
3 chicken portions
1 medium onion, sliced
2 hard-boiled eggs
a little milk
50 g/2 oz butter
50 g/2 oz flour
225 g/8 oz chopped mixed vegetables
pinch of ground nutmeg
salt and pepper to taste
3 tablespoons single cream
225 g/8 oz puff pastry
1 egg, beaten

AMERICAN
½ cup packed quick cooking macaroni
3 chicken portions
1 medium onion, sliced
2 hard-boiled eggs
a little milk
¼ cup butter
½ cup flour
1⅓ cups chopped mixed vegetables
dash of ground nutmeg
salt and pepper to taste
3 tablespoons light cream
½ lb puff pastry
1 egg, beaten

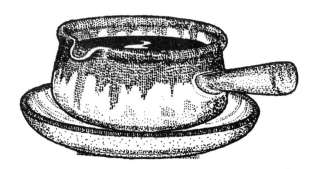

Cook the macaroni in boiling salted water and drain well. Place the chicken and the onion in 600 ml/1 pint/2½ cups salted water and poach for about 20 minutes, or until just tender. Cut the eggs into slices. When the chicken is cooked remove the flesh from the bones. Measure the chicken liquid and make up to 600 ml/1 pint/2½ cups with milk. Melt the butter and stir in the flour, and gradually add the milk liquid with the cooked onion and bring to the boil, stirring constantly. Simmer for 1 minute. Carefully stir in the cooked macaroni, chicken meat, mixed vegetables, nutmeg, salt, pepper and cream. Place the mixture in a 1 litre/1¾ pint/4½ cup deep ovenproof dish and allow to become quite cold. Roll out the pastry, and use to cover the pie. Decorate with the pastry trimmings and brush evenly with the beaten egg. Make a small hole in the centre of the pie and bake in a hot oven (220°C, 425°F, Gas Mark 7) for 15 minutes, then reduce the heat to moderate (180°C, 350°F, Gas Mark 4) and cook for a further 25–30 minutes, until well risen and golden brown.   *Serves 4–5. If frozen, reheat.*

Cranberry chicken bake ✳

METRIC/IMPERIAL
175 g/6 oz dried haricot beans
1 chicken stock cube
300 ml/½ pint boiling water
4 chicken portions
2 tablespoons seasoned flour
50 g/2 oz butter
225 g/8 oz fresh cranberries
75 g/3 oz sugar
1 small onion, chopped
grated zest of 1 orange
150 ml/¼ pint orange juice
½ teaspoon ground mixed spice
salt and pepper to taste

AMERICAN
scant 1 cup navy beans
1 chicken bouillon cube
1¼ cups boiling water
4 chicken portions
2 tablespoons seasoned flour
¼ cup butter
2 cups fresh cranberries
⅓ cup sugar
1 small onion, chopped
grated rind of 1 orange
½ cup orange juice
½ teaspoon ground mixed spice
salt and pepper to taste

Soak the beans in cold water to cover overnight. Drain well, and place in a medium ovenproof casserole. Dissolve the stock cube in the boiling water. Pour over the beans, cover and cook in a moderate oven (180°C, 350°F, Gas Mark 4) for 30 minutes. Meanwhile, coat the chicken portions in seasoned flour. Melt the butter, add the chicken portions and fry until golden brown on all sides. Remove the casserole from the oven and place the chicken portions on top of the beans. Mix together the cranberries, sugar, chopped onion, grated orange zest and orange juice in a saucepan. Bring to the boil and pour over the chicken. Sprinkle with any remaining flour, the spice and add salt and pepper to taste. Cover and return to the oven for a further 45 minutes, or until the chicken is tender. Uncover after 30 minutes and add a little more water if all the juices have been absorbed.   *Serves 4.* If frozen, reheat.

Creamy chicken with vermouth ✳

(Illustrated on page 37)

METRIC/IMPERIAL	AMERICAN
3 lb chicken	*3 lb chicken*
150 ml/¼ pint vermouth	*½ cup vermouth*
150 ml/¼ pint water	*¾ cup water*
2 medium onions, chopped	*2 medium onions, chopped*
salt and black pepper to taste	*salt and black pepper to taste*
about 450 ml/¾ pint milk	*about 2 cups milk*
50 g/2 oz butter	*¼ cup butter*
50 g/2 oz flour	*½ cup flour*
12 stuffed green olives, sliced	*12 stuffed green olives, sliced*
4 slices white bread, diced	*4 slices white bread, diced*
oil for frying	*oil for frying*

Put the chicken into a large ovenproof casserole. Add the vermouth, water and onion and season to taste with salt and black pepper. Cover and cook in a moderate oven (180°C, 350°F, Gas Mark 4) for 1¼ hours or until the chicken is tender. Lift out chicken and allow to cool. Strain the cooking liquid into a measuring jug, skim off any fat and make up to 750 ml/1¼ pints/3 cups with the milk. Remove the flesh from the chicken and cut into bite-sized pieces. Melt the butter in a large pan, stir in the flour and cook for 2 minutes. Gradually add the milk mixture and bring to the boil, stirring constantly, until thickened. Cook for 2 minutes. Taste and adjust the seasoning. Carefully stir in the chicken pieces and sliced olives. Fry the bread dice golden brown in a little oil. Return the chicken mixture to the casserole and cover with the fried bread dice. Reheat in the oven for 10 minutes.   *Serves 4–6.* If frozen, reheat and add bread dice when serving. *Note :* Serve with pasta shells, tossed in butter and sprinkled with paprika.

Pork with mushrooms and rice ✳

METRIC/IMPERIAL	AMERICAN
50 g/2 oz butter	*¼ cup butter*
2 spring onions, chopped	*2 scallions, chopped*
¾ kg/1½ lb lean pork, diced	*3 cups diced lean pork*
225 g/8 oz button mushrooms, sliced	*2 cups sliced button mushrooms*
225 g/8 oz long grain rice	*generous 1 cup long grain rice*
700 ml/1¼ pints chicken stock	*3 cups chicken broth*
salt and pepper to taste	*salt and pepper to taste*

Melt the butter and use to sauté the chopped onion and diced pork until the pork is pale golden on all sides. Add the sliced mushrooms and cook for a further 3 minutes. Place the rice in the bottom of a buttered medium ovenproof casserole. Spoon over the pork, onion and mushroom mixture, pour over the stock and season. Cover and bake in a moderate oven (180°C, 350°F, Gas Mark 4) for 1 hour.   *Serves 4.* If frozen, reheat.

OPPOSITE : *Hungarian beef in red wine with baked potatoes and college salad.*

PAGE *36 : Danish club streaky, with rice salad and chocolate and ginger date pudding.*

PAGE *37 Creamy chicken with vermouth, paprika pasta shells and rich fruit supper scone.*

Baked pork with mandarins

METRIC/IMPERIAL	AMERICAN
4 thick pork chops	*4 thick pork chops*
225 g/8 oz long grain rice	*generous 1 cup long grain rice*
311 g/11 oz can mandarin oranges	*11 oz can mandarin oranges*
450 g/¾ pint chicken stock	*2 cups chicken broth*
½ teaspoon dried sage or basil	*½ teaspoon dried sage or basil*
salt and pepper to taste	*salt and pepper to taste*

Fry the pork chops without any fat until golden on both sides. Place the rice in the bottom of a shallow ovenproof dish and arrange the chops on top. Drain the oranges and scatter over the chops. Mix together the mandarin syrup and the stock and pour into the dish. Sprinkle with the herbs and seasoning to taste. Cover with lid or foil and bake in a moderate oven (180°C, 350°F, Gas Mark 4) for 45 minutes.   *Serves 4.*

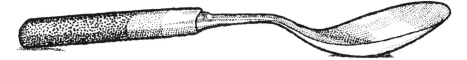

Lamb's liver casserole ✳

METRIC/IMPERIAL	AMERICAN
50 g/2 oz butter or dripping	*¼ cup butter or drippings*
2 rashers streaky bacon	*2 slices bacon*
2 large onions, sliced	*2 large onions, sliced*
2 large potatoes, sliced	*2 large potatoes, sliced*
¾ kg/1 ½ lb lamb's liver in one piece	*1½ lb lamb's liver in one piece*
25 g/1 oz flour	*¼ cup flour*
396 g/14 oz can tomatoes	*14 oz can tomatoes*
2 tablespoons sherry	*2 tablespoons sherry*
salt and pepper to taste	*salt and pepper to taste*
grated zest of 1 lemon	*grated rind of 1 lemon*
1 bouquet garni	*1 bouquet garni*

Melt the butter or dripping in a frying pan. Cut the bacon into 2 cm/¾ inch pieces and fry in the hot fat for about 1 minute. Add the onion and potato and fry, stirring, for about 3 minutes. Remove the bacon and vegetables from the fat with a slotted draining spoon, and place in a large ovenproof casserole. Gently brown the liver on all sides in the remaining fat and place on top of the vegetables. Add the flour to the remaining juices in the frying pan and cook, stirring constantly, for 3 minutes. Gradually add the liquid from the can of tomatoes and bring to the boil, stirring all the time until the mixture thickens. Add the sherry and sufficient water, if necessary, to make a smooth gravy. Season well and stir in the lemon zest. Roughly chop the tomatoes and spoon round the liver. Add the gravy and bouquet garni. Cover and cook in a cool oven (150°C, 300°F, Gas Mark 2) for 2 hours. Remove the bouquet garni and slice the liver before serving. *Serves 4–6*. If frozen, reheat covered.

A selection of pies : clockwise from the front, *country chicken pie, lamb pie with pears and saucy fish pie.*

Kidney stew with bacon dumplings ✳

METRIC/IMPERIAL	AMERICAN
¾ kg/1½ lb ox kidney	1½ lb beef kidney
25 g/1 oz flour	¼ cup flour
½ teaspoon salt	½ teaspoon salt
pinch of pepper	dash of pepper
¼ teaspoon hot paprika pepper	¼ teaspoon hot paprika pepper
2 tablespoons oil	2 tablespoons oil
1 medium onion, chopped	1 medium onion, chopped
2 medium carrots, chopped	2 medium carrots, chopped
250 ml/½ pint beef stock	1¼ cups beef broth
2 tablespoons sherry	2 tablespoons sherry

bacon dumplings:

2 rashers streaky bacon	2 slices bacon
100 g/4 oz plain flour	1 cup all-purpose flour
2 teaspoons baking powder	2 teaspoons baking powder
½ teaspoon salt	½ teaspoon salt
100 ml/4 fl oz milk	½ cup milk
1 tablespoon oil	1 tablespoon oil

Skin, core and dice the kidney. Season the flour with the salt, pepper and paprika pepper and use to coat the kidney pieces. Heat the oil in a heavy pan and brown the kidney well, then add the onion and carrot. Sauté for 3 minutes, then stir in the beef stock and sherry. Transfer to a large ovenproof casserole, cover and cook in a moderate oven (170°C, 325°F, Gas Mark 3) for 1½ hours. Meanwhile, prepare the bacon dumplings. Derind the bacon, cut into small dice and fry until crisp. Drain on absorbent paper. Sift the flour, baking powder and salt into a bowl. Make a well in the centre, add the milk, oil and fried bacon pieces and stir lightly with a fork until the flour is moistened. Drop spoonfuls on the simmering stew, cover and return to the oven for 20 minutes. Serve immediately. *Serves 6*. If frozen, reheat. Make dumplings and add to stew when very hot.

Ham and mushroom crumble ✳

METRIC/IMPERIAL	AMERICAN
225 g/8 oz mushrooms, sliced	½ lb mushrooms, sliced
150 g/5 oz butter or margarine	generous ½ cup butter or margarine
salt and pepper to taste	salt and pepper to taste
450 g/1 lb tomatoes	1 lb tomatoes
225 g/8 oz ham, diced	½ lb ham, diced
225 g/8 oz flour	2 cups flour
100 g/4 oz strong Cheddar cheese, grated	1 cup grated sharp Cheddar cheese

Place the mushrooms in the bottom of a deep ovenproof dish. Take 25 g/1 oz/2 tablespoons of the butter and dot over the mushrooms. Season well. Skin and slice the tomatoes and add these to the dish. Place the ham on top of the tomatoes. Rub the remaining butter well into the flour. Add salt, and the grated cheese and stir to mix thoroughly. Heap the crumble on top of the dish and bake in a hot oven (220°C, 425°F, Gas Mark 7) for about 25 minutes. *Serves 4*. If frozen, reheat.

Danish club streaky
(illustrated on page 36)

METRIC/IMPERIAL	AMERICAN
1½/–1¾ kg/3–4 lb piece streaky bacon	3–4 lb piece slab bacon
100 g/4 oz dried sage and onion stuffing mix	1 cup herb-seasoned stuffing mix
1 teaspoon ground bay leaves	1 teaspoon ground bay leaves
2 tablespoons chopped parsley	2 tablespoons chopped parsley
2 tablespoons seedless raisins	2 tablespoons seedless raisins
salt and pepper to taste	salt and pepper to taste
1 egg, beaten	1 egg, beaten
2 tablespoons soft brown sugar	2 tablespoons light brown sugar
sprigs of watercress	sprigs of watercress

Divide the piece of bacon in half. Put the 2 pieces in a large pan with cold water to cover and bring slowly to the boil. Drain both pieces and remove the rind. Place the stuffing mix in a small bowl, add the spice, herbs, raisins and salt and pepper to taste and pour in just sufficient boiling water to make a very stiff mixture. Beat in the egg. Sandwich together the pieces of bacon with the stuffing mix and tie with white string in 2 places. Score the top fat and place the stuffed joint in a large ovenproof casserole. Cover and cook in a moderate oven (180°C, 350°F, Gas Mark 4) for 2–2½ hours, according to weight. Remove the lid, cut through the string and pull away from the top. Sprinkle the joint with the brown sugar and return to the oven for 10–15 minutes, to brown and glaze the top. Remove carefully and serve on an ovenproof platter, garnished with sprigs of watercress and accompanied by hot brown rolls or thick slices of fresh brown bread. *Serves 4 hot and 4–6 cold.*

Oven baked potato dishes with a difference: When you are cooking a main meal in the oven, use up space and oven heat with appetising and unusual potato dishes.

Potato goulash

METRIC/IMPERIAL	AMERICAN
225 g/8 oz onions, chopped	*2 cups chopped onion*
50 g/2 oz butter	*¼ cup butter*
¾ kg/1¾ lb potatoes	*1¾ lb potatoes*
½ teaspoon caraway seeds	*½ teaspoon caraway seeds*
1 teaspoon mild paprika pepper	*1 teaspoon mild paprika pepper*
¼ teaspoon dried marjoram	*¼ teaspoon dried marjoram*
175 ml/6 fl oz chicken stock	*¾ cup chicken broth*

Lightly fry the onion in the butter. Transfer to a small ovenproof casserole. Thinly slice the potatoes and layer in the casserole with the caraway seeds, paprika, marjoram and salt to taste. Pour in the stock, cover and cook in a moderately hot oven (200°C, 400°F, Gas Mark 6) for 1 hour.   *Serves 4–6.*

Baked creamed potatoes

METRIC/IMPERIAL	AMERICAN
¾ kg/1½ lb potatoes, sliced	*1½ lb potatoes, sliced*
250 ml/8 fl oz milk	*1 cup milk*
25 g/1 oz butter	*2 tablespoons butter*

Place the sliced potato in a small ovenproof casserole. Add the milk, butter and salt and pepper to taste. Cover and bake in a moderately hot oven (200°C, 400°F, Gas Mark 6) for 1 hour. Remove the lid and beat the potato with a fork until creamy.   *Serves 4.*

Swiss roast potatoes   *(illustrated on page 38)*

METRIC/IMPERIAL	AMERICAN
4 large potatoes	*4 large potatoes*
2 medium onions	*2 medium onions*
25 g/1 oz butter	*2 tablespoons butter*
150 ml/¼ pint soured cream	*½ cup soured cream*
½ teaspoon ground nutmeg	*½ teaspoon ground nutmeg*

Boil the potatoes in their skins until just tender. Cool, peel and roughly grate the potatoes and place in a small ovenproof casserole. Finely chop the onions and fry lightly in the butter. Spoon over the grated potato. Season the soured cream with the nutmeg and salt to taste and pour over the potato mixture. Cover and cook in a moderately hot oven (200°C, 400°F, Gas Mark 6) for 40 minutes.   *Serves 4–6.*

Chapter 2
Oven to table dinner parties

The most flattering invitation you can extend to your friends is probably an invitation to dinner, and here is a real opportunity to shine as a hostess. Composing the menu gives your imagination plenty of scope, but do not let it run away with you. Culinary daydreams are great fun but it is more important to plan a meal with just a few courses which contrast effectively in terms of flavour, texture and colour. Equally important, choose one that you can budget for comfortably and prepare easily in the length of time you have available.

Some dishes are particularly sensitive to a last-minute delay in sitting down to table. The choice of a hot soufflé for the first course might become an error of some magnitude if your guests arrive late or cannot tear themselves away from the pre-dinner drinks.

Three well-chosen courses

A nicely balanced meal probably includes one course served cold, which simplifies the choice of either the starter or the sweet. If the main course is particularly rich, try to choose light, delicate dishes to precede and follow it. If one dish involves long and complicated preparation, the others should be straight-forward. Three courses are now usually considered suffi-

cient for modern tastes. After these, a cheese board or a finger savoury will defeat most appetites and leave no enthusiasm for the thinnest of chocolate mints or daintiest of *petits fours* with the coffee.

At all costs avoid a frantic clash of saucepans or the fretful whine of the mixer after your guests have arrived. If one course is ready to serve cold, and the others can be confidently produced from the oven when required, you need experience no panic. Then the dinner party will be an ideal social occasion, one which the hostess enjoys in a relaxed manner along with her guests.

For this reason, the menus given here offer original ideas for elegant dinner parties without toil or fuss, planned to employ the oven for all but preliminary cooking. Once your cold dish has been prepared and served to the point of awaiting the final garnish or decoration, the rest of the cooking is completed in the oven, in dishes which will go straight to the table. Hot soup is the exception. Served out into pre-heated stoneware soup dishes and covered, it can await the diners for some time without cooling down. Some of the starters are simple but highly unusual, and would make a pleasant talking point to get conversation round the table going. All the following menus serve 4, but quantities can be increased if necessary.

Menu	*Jamaican grapefruit*
	Lamb chops Adriana
	Souffléed pasta shells
	Rice salad
	Baked macaroon apples

Jamaican grapefruit

(Illustrated on page 55)

Cut two grapefruit in half and loosen the segments. Sprinkle each half with brown sugar, add a knob of butter and 1 teaspoon of rum. Place in small ovenproof dishes and cook in a moderate oven (180°C, 350°F, Gas Mark 4) for 20 minutes. Serve hot with a small piece of stem ginger in the centre of each grapefruit half.

Lamb chops Adriana

METRIC/IMPERIAL	AMERICAN
8 lamb chops	*8 lamb chops*
seasoned flour	*seasoned flour*
25 g/1 oz butter	*2 tablespoons butter*
1 small onion	*1 small onion*
100 g/4 oz button mushrooms, sliced	*1 cup sliced button mushrooms*
225 g/8 oz can tomatoes	*1 cup canned tomatoes*
1 tablespoon dark chunky marmalade	*1 tablespoon dark chunky marmalade*
salt and pepper to taste	*salt and pepper to taste*

Trim the chops and coat with seasoned flour. Heat the butter in a pan and use to fry the chops on both sides until golden. Transfer to a medium ovenproof casserole. Finely chop the onion and fry in the remaining fat until soft. Add the sliced mushrooms, tomatoes and their liquid and the marmalade. Mix well and pour over the chops. Cook in a moderate oven (180°C, 350°F, Gas Mark 4) for 20–25 minutes. Taste and adjust seasoning as necessary.

Souffléed pasta shells

METRIC/IMPERIAL	AMERICAN
3 tablespoons oil	*3 tablespoons oil*
175 g/6 oz pasta shells	*1¼ cups pasta shells*
2 eggs, separated	*2 eggs, separated*
300 ml/½ pint hot savoury white sauce	*1¼ cups hot savory white sauce*
salt and pepper to taste	*salt and pepper to taste*

Bring a large pan of lightly salted water to the boil, add the oil and gradually stir in the pasta shells. Cook uncovered for 6 minutes or until just tender, then drain well. Beat the egg yolks into the hot sauce. Gently fold in the cooked pasta and add extra seasoning if necessary. Whisk the egg whites until stiff and fold into the pasta mixture only until well combined. Turn into a greased shallow ovenproof dish and bake in a moderate oven (180°C, 350°F, Gas Mark 4) for 40–45 minutes, until slightly risen and golden brown.

Rice salad
(Illustrated on page 36)

METRIC/IMPERIAL	AMERICAN
100 g/4 oz cooked long grain rice	*⅔ cup cooked long grain rice*
4 tomatoes, skinned	*4 tomatoes, skinned*
75 g/2¾ oz canned pimento	*¼ cup sliced canned pimento*
1 clove garlic, crushed	*1 clove garlic, crushed*
1 small onion	*1 small onion*
French dressing	*Italian dressing*
chopped parsley	*chopped parsley*

Combine the cooked rice, quartered tomatoes, sliced pimentoes, with liquid from the can, and the crushed garlic. Finely chop the onion and add with just sufficient dressing to coat all the ingredients. Toss together lightly and serve sprinkled with chopped parsley.

Baked macaroon apples
(Illustrated on page 58)

METRIC/IMPERIAL	AMERICAN
4 cooking apples	*4 baking apples*
2 tablespoons seedless raisins	*2 tablespoons seedless raisins*
2 tablespoons sultanas	*2 tablespoons golden raisins*
1 tablespoon chopped glacé cherries	*1 tablespoon chopped candied cherries*
15 g/½ oz butter	*1 tablespoon butter*
lemon juice	*lemon juice*
topping:	
50 g/2 oz ground almonds	*½ cup ground almonds*
100 g/4 oz sugar	*½ cup sugar*
2 teaspoons cornflour	*2 teaspoons cornstarch*
1 egg white	*1 egg white*
vanilla essence	*vanilla extract*
4 glacé cherries	*4 candied cherries*

Core the apples and peel away a slice of skin round the centres to prevent the apples from bursting. Arrange in a buttered shallow ovenproof dish. Mix together the raisins, sultanas and chopped glacé cherries and use to fill the centre of each apple. Put a little butter on top of each and sprinkle with lemon juice. Bake in a moderate oven (180°C, 350°F, Gas Mark 4) for 20 minutes. While the apples are cooking, make the macaroon mixture. Mix together the ground almonds, sugar and cornflour. Stiffly whisk the egg white, add a few drops of vanilla essence and combine with the almond mixture. Remove the apples from the oven and spoon the macaroon mixture over them. Return to the oven for a further 20 minutes. Top each apple with a cherry.

<table>
<tr><td>

Menu

</td><td>

Smoked mackerel with tomato horseradish cream
Pork chops with artichoke hearts
Potatoes baked in stock
Raw mushroom salad
Apple and nut pudding

</td></tr>
</table>

Smoked mackerel with tomato horseradish cream

Allow 1 small fillet of smoked mackerel for each person. Blend together 4 tablespoons horseradish sauce, 1 teaspoon tomato purée (paste), and 2 tablespoons whipped cream. Serve the mackerel with the sauce accompanied by thin rolls of brown bread and butter.

Pork chops with artichoke hearts ✱

METRIC/IMPERIAL	AMERICAN
4 pork chops	*4 pork chops*
1 tablespoon seasoned flour	*1 tablespoon seasoned flour*
150 ml/¼ pint soured cream	*½ cup soured cream*
1 tablespoon lemon juice	*1 tablespoon lemon juice*
½ teaspoon grated lemon zest	*½ teaspoon grated lemon rind*
1 teaspoon sugar	*1 teaspoon sugar*
½ teaspoon dried thyme	*½ teaspoon dried thyme*
salt and pepper to taste	*salt and pepper to taste*
6 tablespoons water	*⅓ cup water*
396 g/14 oz can artichoke hearts	*14 oz can artichoke hearts*

Trim the chops and remove any surplus fat. Coat with seasoned flour. Brown lightly on each side in melted surplus pork fat. Transfer to an oblong ovenproof dish. Mix together the soured cream, lemon juice, lemon zest, sugar, thyme and seasoning. Dilute with the water and pour over the chops. Drain the artichoke hearts and arrange round the chops. Cover with lid or foil and cook in a moderate oven (180°C, 350°F, Gas Mark 4) for about 30 minutes, or until the chops are tender. If frozen, reheat.

Raw mushroom salad

Remove the stalks from 24 small button mushrooms. Cut them into thin slices and arrange in a shallow dish. Pour over just sufficient French (Italian) dressing to moisten and toss carefully. Chill for at least 30 minutes and serve sprinkled with chopped chives and chopped parsley.

Potatoes baked in stock

METRIC/IMPERIAL
$\frac{3}{4}$ kg/1$\frac{1}{2}$ lb potatoes, sliced
150 ml/$\frac{1}{4}$ pint stock
50 g/2 oz butter, melted
salt and pepper to taste

AMERICAN
1$\frac{1}{2}$ lb potatoes, sliced
generous $\frac{1}{2}$ cup broth
$\frac{1}{4}$ cup melted butter
salt and pepper to taste

Place the sliced potato in a small ovenproof casserole. Add the stock and melted butter. Add extra seasoning to taste, cover and bake in a moderately hot oven (200°C, 400°F, Gas Mark 6) for 1 hour. *Serves 4.*

Apple and nut pudding

METRIC/IMPERIAL
2 large cooking apples
1 egg
150 g/6 oz sugar
$\frac{1}{2}$ teaspoon vanilla essence
25 g/1 oz butter, melted
50 g/2 oz flour
$\frac{1}{2}$ teaspoon salt
75 g/3 oz mixed nuts, chopped

AMERICAN
2 large baking apples
1 egg
$\frac{3}{4}$ cup sugar
$\frac{1}{2}$ teaspoon vanilla extract
2 tablespoons melted butter
$\frac{1}{2}$ cup flour
$\frac{1}{2}$ teaspoon salt
$\frac{3}{4}$ cup chopped mixed nuts

Peel, core and chop the apples. Beat the egg, add sugar, vanilla essence and melted butter and beat thoroughly. Add the apples, flour, salt and nuts. Mix well. Place in a buttered ovenproof dish and cook in a moderate oven (180°C, 350°F, Gas Mark 4) for 30 minutes. Serve with whipped cream or ice cream.

Menu	Avocado and prawn mousse Duck with fruited sauerkraut Whipped almond-crusted potatoes Maraschino meringue gâteau

Avocado and prawn mousse ✳

METRIC/IMPERIAL
1 tablespoon gelatine
150 ml/¼ pint white wine
2 large ripe avocados
150 ml/¼ pint mayonnaise
grated zest of ½ lemon
salt and pepper to taste
150 ml/¼ pint double cream, whipped
100 g/4 oz peeled prawns, chopped
  parsley sprigs

AMERICAN
1 tablespoon unflavored gelatine
½ cup white wine
2 large ripe avocados
½ cup mayonnaise
grated rind of ½ lemon
salt and pepper to taste
½ cup heavy cream, whipped
1 cup shelled shrimp, chopped
  parsley sprigs

Dissolve the gelatine in the white wine in a basin over a pan of hot water. Peel, halve and stone the avocados. Chop the flesh roughly and place in a blender with the dissolved gelatine and wine, mayonnaise, lemon zest and seasoning to taste. Liquidize until smooth. Pour into a bowl and allow to stand. When the mixture is on the point of setting, fold in the whipped cream and the chopped shellfish. Divide the mixture among 4 footed dessert dishes and chill until set. Decorate the mousses with small sprigs of parsley, or with a few extra peeled prawns, if liked. If frozen, defrost in refrigerator.

Duck with fruited sauerkraut

Note : Recipes for duck with orange, or black cherries, are well known. Here is something entirely different.

METRIC/IMPERIAL
2¼ kg/5 lb duck
onion salt and pepper to taste
150 ml/¼ pint Riesling (or other dry
  white wine)
2 bay leaves
1 kg/2 lb canned sauerkraut
6 tablespoons pineapple syrup
3 tablespoons duck fat
2 tablespoons flour
100 g/4 oz drained canned pineapple
  chunks

AMERICAN
5 lb duck
onion salt and pepper to taste
generous ½ cup dry white wine

2 bay leaves
2 lb canned sauerkraut
6 tablespoons pineapple syrup
3 tablespoons duck fat
2 tablespoons flour
¾ cup drained canned pineapple
  chunks

Sprinkle the duck with salt and pepper inside and out. Place in an oblong ovenproof dish and roast in a moderately hot oven (200°C, 400°F, Gas Mark 6) for 1 hour and 20 minutes. Remove from the dish, strain off the fat and reserve. Place the wine and bay leaves in a saucepan and boil until reduced by half. Drain the sauerkraut and add the liquid to the wine with the pineapple syrup. Carve the duck into serving portions, and reserve the juices which run from it. In another saucepan, melt the duck fat and stir in the flour. Gradually add the strained wine and the juices from the duck and bring to the boil, stirring. Season, place the sauerkraut in the base of the ovenproof dish, pour the sauce over and cover with the pineapple chunks. Arrange the duck portions over this, skin side uppermost, and return to the oven for a further 30 minutes, until the duck is rich brown and the sauerkraut is soft.   *Serves 4–6.*

Whipped almond-crusted potatoes ✳

Mash $\frac{1}{2}$ kg/1$\frac{1}{4}$ lb cooked floury potatoes with 2 egg yolks, a little butter and milk and season with ground nutmeg, salt and pepper. Whisk 2 egg whites until stiff and fold into the potato mixture. Spread in a buttered shallow ovenproof dish and sprinkle the surface generously with flaked (slivered) almonds. Drizzle over a little melted butter and place on a shelf in the warmest part of the oven for 20–25 minutes, until slightly risen and the almonds are golden brown. If frozen, reheat.

Maraschino meringue gâteau

METRIC/IMPERIAL	AMERICAN
4 egg whites	4 egg whites
165 g/6 oz soft brown sugar	$\frac{3}{4}$ cup light brown sugar
50 g/2 oz castor sugar	$\frac{1}{4}$ cup granulated sugar
300 ml/$\frac{1}{2}$ pint whipping cream	1$\frac{1}{4}$ cups whipping cream
1 tablespoon maraschino syrup	1 tablespoon maraschino syrup
3 tablespoons chopped maraschino cherries	3 tablespoons chopped maraschino cherries
25 g/1 oz crushed macaroons	$\frac{1}{4}$ cup crushed macaroons

Cover 3 large ovenproof plates with lightly oiled foil, or use non-stick vegetable parchment. Mark 3 circles 17·5 cm/7 in in diameter using a plate as a guide, and taking care not to tear the foil. Whisk the egg whites until soft peaks form. Whisk in the brown sugar and continue whisking until the meringue stands in firm glossy peaks. Fold in the castor sugar. Divide among the 3 plates. Bake in a very cool oven (110°C, 225°F, Gas Mark $\frac{1}{4}$) for 2$\frac{1}{2}$–3 hours, until quite dry. If you use foil, peel it away while the meringue layers are still warm and cool them on a wire tray. Whip the cream until it forms peaks, then whip in the maraschino syrup and fold in the chopped cherries and crushed macaroons. Sandwich the layers together with the filling, on a serving plate. Serve chilled and cut into wedges.   *Serves 4–6.*

<table>
<tr><td>Menu</td><td>*Grapefruit and avocado starter*
Heavenly beef
Buttered ribbon noodles
Chinese leaf salad
Coffee bread ice cream</td></tr>
</table>

Complete menu illustrated on pages 56–57.

Grapefruit and avocado starter

Peel and segment 1 large juicy grapefruit. Halve, peel and slice 1 large ripe avocado pear. Make a dressing with 2 tablespoons white wine, 2 tablespoons corn oil, a pinch each of castor sugar, salt and pepper, and shake well together. Carefully combine the grapefruit segments and avocado slices with the dressing and serve in lettuce leaf cups on small plates.

Heavenly beef ✱

METRIC/IMPERIAL	AMERICAN
$\frac{1}{2}$ kg/1$\frac{1}{4}$ lb thickly sliced topside of beef	1$\frac{1}{4}$ lb thickly sliced rump of beef
6 tablespoons soy sauce	6 tablespoons soy sauce
6 tablespoons dry white wine	6 tablespoons dry white wine
1 tablespoon sugar	1 tablespoon sugar
1$\frac{1}{2}$ teaspoons ground ginger	1$\frac{1}{2}$ teaspoons ground ginger
2 cloves of garlic, crushed	2 cloves of garlic, crushed
6 spring onions	6 scallions

Cut the meat into thin strips and place in a shallow ovenproof dish. Mix together the soy sauce, wine, sugar, ginger and garlic and pour over the beef strips. Cover the dish and allow to stand in a cool place for about 4 hours. Uncover and bake in a moderate oven (180°C, 350°F, Gas Mark 4) for 30 minutes, basting twice with the marinade.

Meanwhile, make the spring onion curls. Trim the onions to a length of 5 cm/2 in, slice through from the top 5 or 6 times halfway down the onions and drop into a bowl of iced water until the cut surfaces curl. Drain well. Serve the beef and sauce on a bed of buttered ribbon noodles and garnish with the onion curls. If frozen, cook noodles and prepare garnish while beef reheats.

Buttered ribbon noodles

Cook 225 g/8 oz noodles in plenty of boiling salted water, with 1 tablespoon oil to keep the strands separate. Drain, rinse well with fresh hot water through a colander and drain again. Meanwhile, put 50 g/2 oz/¼ cup butter in a small ovenproof casserole. Cover and place in a moderate oven (180°C, 350°F, Gas Mark 4) until melted. Add the noodles and toss with 2 forks to coat the strands. Sprinkle with garlic salt and freshly ground black pepper to taste. Cover and return to the oven for a further 10 minutes, to heat through.

Chinese leaf salad

Use the upper halves of the leaves, reserving the broad-ribbed base of the head for cooking. Wash and finely shred the leaves and place in a salad bowl. Prepare a dressing, using 4 tablespoons pineapple juice, 2 tablespoons oil and seasoning to taste. Pour over the shredded leaves and toss lightly. Serve scattered with washed mustard and cress.

Coffee bread ice cream

METRIC/IMPERIAL	AMERICAN
600 ml/1 pint double cream	*2½ cups heavy cream*
150 ml/¼ pint strong black coffee	*½ cup strong black coffee*
100 g/4 oz castor sugar	*½ cup granulated sugar*
4 egg yolks	*4 egg yolks*
50 g/2 oz toasted breadcrumbs	*4 tablespoons toasted breadcrumbs*

Put the cream into the top of a double boiler and bring just to the boil. Add the coffee. Whisk the castor sugar with the egg yolks and gradually whisk in the cream and coffee. Return the mixture to the top of the double boiler. Stir over gentle heat until the mixture thickens. Pour into 6 footed dessert dishes and sprinkle the surfaces with toasted bread-crumbs. Freeze until firm and serve with sponge fingers.   *Serves 6.*

Menu	*Consommé Julienne*
	Chicken in a creamy peach sauce
	Hot savoury scones with butter
	(see page 90)
	Petits pois with sweetcorn
	Lettuce heart and bean sprout salad
	Baked marmalade bananas

Consommé Julienne * *(Illustrated on page 55)*

Place 1 chicken breast portion in a medium ovenproof casserole and pour over 900 ml/ 1½ pints/4 cups hot strong chicken stock (broth). Add a bouquet garni and season to taste with white pepper and onion salt. Cover and cook in a moderate oven (180°C, 350°F, Gas Mark 4) for 45 minutes to 1 hour. Pour through a fine sieve into a fairly large saucepan. Discard the chicken and bouquet garni. Allow the consommé to cool and skim off any surplus fat. Add 1 medium carrot and 1 stick of celery, cut into Julienne strips. Return to the heat, bring to the boil and simmer for 5 minutes. Remove from the heat and serve in 4 covered soup coupes. If frozen, add garnish while reheating.

Chicken in a creamy peach sauce

METRIC/IMPERIAL	AMERICAN
425 g/15 oz can peach slices	*15 oz can peach slices*
4 chicken portions	*4 chicken portions*
1 onion, chopped	*1 onion, chopped*
salt and pepper to taste	*salt and pepper to taste*
50 g/2 oz butter	*¼ cup butter*
50 g/2 oz flour	*½ cup all-purpose flour*
300 ml/½ pint medium dry white wine	*1¼ cups medium dry white wine*
300 ml/½ pint chicken stock	*1¼ cups chicken broth*
175 g/6 oz Gouda cheese, grated	*1½ cups grated Gouda cheese*
4 tablespoons peach brandy	*4 tablespoons peach brandy*
6 tablespoons single cream	*6 tablespoons light cream*
2 tablespoons chopped parsley	*2 tablespoons chopped parsley*

Drain the peach slices and reserve the syrup. Place the chicken portions, chopped onion and peach slices in an ovenproof dish. Season with salt and pepper and cover with lid or foil. Bake in a moderately hot oven (190°C, 375°F, Gas Mark 5) for 40 minutes. Meanwhile, make the sauce. Place the butter, flour, wine and stock in a saucepan. Bring to the boil, whisking all the time, and simmer for 2 minutes. Remove from the heat and stir in two-thirds of the cheese and 6 tablespoons of the reserved peach syrup. Strain any juices from the dish of chicken into the sauce. Add the brandy and cream, stir well, and season to taste. Pour the sauce over the chicken and sprinkle with the remaining cheese. Return the dish to the oven for a further 15 minutes. Sprinkle with chopped parsley before serving.

Petits pois with sweetcorn

Carefully wash the outer leaves of 2 lettuces (reserving the hearts for the lettuce heart salad). Shred and place in a buttered small ovenproof casserole. Drain a 198 g/7 oz can of sweetcorn kernels and mix with 225 g/8 oz/½ lb frozen petits pois (small peas). Spoon the vegetables into the casserole in three layers, sprinkling a tablespoon of finely chopped spring onion (scallion) and seasoning to taste over each layer. Finish by drizzling 25 g/1 oz/2 tablespoons melted butter over the top. Cover and place on a shelf in the warmest part of the oven for 30 minutes.

Lettuce heart and bean sprout salad

Divide the hearts of 2 lettuces into 4, making 8 quarters in all. Finely chop 100 g/4 oz/ ¼ lb bean sprouts. Make a dressing using 1 teaspoon grated lemon zest (rind), 1 table-spoon lemon juice, 2 tablespoons oil, ½ teaspoon salt, ½ teaspoon sugar and ¼ teaspoon pepper. Shake well in a screw-topped container to blend, then pour over the chopped bean sprouts and toss lightly. Divide the dressed bean sprouts among 4 small bowls and top each with 2 lettuce heart quarters. (A home-grown mixture of sprouting seeds could be used instead of the bean sprouts.)

Baked marmalade bananas *(illustrated on front of jacket)*

METRIC/IMPERIAL
225 g/8 oz marmalade
150 ml/¼ pint white wine
grated zest and juice of 1 lemon
2 tablespoons soft brown sugar
6 large firm bananas
25 g/1 oz flaked almonds

AMERICAN
½ lb marmalade
½ cup white wine
grated rind and juice of 1 lemon
2 tablespoons light brown sugar
6 large firm bananas
¼ cup slivered almonds

Put the marmalade into a pan with the wine, lemon zest and juice, and the brown sugar. Stir over gentle heat until the sugar has dissolved, and the marmalade melted. Simmer for 10 minutes. Arrange the bananas in a shallow ovenproof dish. Spoon the marmalade and lemon sauce over the bananas and sprinkle with the almonds. Bake in a moderately hot oven (190°C, 375°F, Gas Mark 5) for 20 minutes. Serve hot, with cream.

Menu	*Melon and grape starter* *Halibut with lemony mushroom sauce* *Cheese-baked potatoes (see page 86)* *Buttered spinach* *Mulled fruit salad* *Chicken livers and bacon rolls on toast*

Melon and grape starter
(Illustrated on page 55)

Cut the top from a ripe ogen (cantaloupe) melon and remove the seeds. Using a melon baller, scoop out as many balls as possible and reserve. Scrape out remaining melon flesh and juice, and divide among 4 wine glasses. Peel and remove the seeds from 225 g/8 oz/ $\frac{1}{2}$ lb large black or purple grapes. Mix together the grapes and melon balls and spoon into the glasses. Pour 1 tablespoon port over each glass of fruit and allow to stand for at least 10 minutes before serving.

Halibut with lemony mushroom sauce

METRIC/IMPERIAL	AMERICAN
4 halibut steaks	*4 halibut steaks*
50 g/2 oz butter	*$\frac{1}{4}$ cup butter*
100 g/4 oz mushrooms, sliced	*$\frac{1}{4}$ lb mushrooms, sliced*
pinch of ground nutmeg	*dash of ground nutmeg*
2 teaspoons finely grated lemon zest	*2 teaspoons finely grated lemon rind*
1 tablespoon chopped parsley	*1 tablespoon chopped parsley*
150 ml/$\frac{1}{4}$ pint soured cream	*$\frac{1}{2}$ cup soured cream*
salt and pepper to taste	*salt and pepper to taste*

Arrange the fish steaks in a greased oval ovenproof dish. Dot with half the butter and cover with foil. Bake in a moderate oven (180°C, 350°F, Gas Mark 4) for 15 minutes. Meanwhile, melt the remaining butter and use to sauté the sliced mushroom until golden brown. Add the nutmeg, lemon zest, chopped parsley, juices drained from the fish and the soured cream. Season to taste. Stir over moderate heat but do not allow to boil. Pour the sauce over the fish and return to the oven for 10 minutes. *Serves 4.*

OPPOSITE: *Chilled cucumber with seasoned cream, consommé julienne, melon and grape starter and Jamaican grapefruit.*

PAGES 56, 57: *A complete dinner party menu for 4: Grapefruit and avocado starter, heavenly beef with buttered ribbon noodles and Chinese leaf salad. To follow, coffee bread ice cream.*

Buttered spinach ✱

Wash and cook 1 kg/2 lb leaf spinach in the water clinging to the leaves and a little salt. Drain off the water, pressing the cooked spinach against the side of the pan with a saucer. Snip up the cooked spinach with kitchen scissors. Pour in 50 g/2 oz/¼ cup melted butter and sprinkle with 1 tablespoon sifted flour. Stir quickly over moderate heat for about 3 minutes, until the flour is cooked. Add ½ teaspoon ground nutmeg and serve very hot. (This recipe can be made with frozen spinach.)

Mulled fruit salad ✱ *(Illustrated on page 58)*

METRIC/IMPERIAL	AMERICAN
600 ml/1 pint cider	*2½ cups cider*
225 g/8 oz sugar	*1 cup sugar*
small piece of cinnamon stick	*small piece of cinnamon stick*
few cloves	*few cloves*
2 apples	*2 apples*
2 pears	*2 pears*
6 apricots	*6 apricots*
6 plums	*6 plums*
2 oranges	*2 oranges*
2 bananas	*2 bananas*
2 tablespoons rum	*2 tablespoons rum*

Put the cider in a pan with the sugar, cinnamon stick and cloves. Stir over gentle heat until the sugar has dissolved then simmer for 15 minutes. Core and thickly slice the apples. Peel, core and thickly slice the pears. Halve and stone the apricots and plums. Remove all the peel and pith from the oranges and cut the flesh into slices. Cut the bananas into thick diagonal slices. Put all the prepared fruit into a medium ovenproof casserole and pour over the strained cider syrup. Cover and cook in a moderate oven (180°C, 350°F, Gas Mark 4) for 45 minutes. Spoon over the rum and serve immediately with cream. *Serves 4 hot and 4 cold.* If frozen, spoon over rum when serving.

   Note : Other fruits in season can be included when making this unusual hot fruit salad. Try adding a few strawberries, seeded grapes, or stoned and quartered peaches.

Chicken livers and bacon rolls on toast

Trim 8 chicken livers. Fry them in 25 g/1 oz/2 tablespoons butter until just firm. Derind 4 rashers (slices) of streaky (side) bacon and divide each in half crossways. Wrap each liver in a piece of bacon, tuck the ends firmly underneath and arrange the rolls in a greased shallow ovenproof dish. Place on a shelf in the warmest part of the oven when you have removed the fish from the oven. Bake the rolls for 35 minutes. After serving the sweet, make 2 slices of toast or fry 2 slices of white bread in bacon fat until golden brown. Cut the slices in half and serve each person with 2 rolls placed on a half-slice of toasted or fried bread. Top with sprigs of parsley.

Mulled fruit salad, peaches under a hazelnut crust with chiffon custard, and baked macaroon apple.

Menu	Chilled cucumber with seasoned cream
	Andalusian chicken with olives
	Gingered rice pilaff
	Torn spinach salad
	Peaches under a hazelnut crust
	Chiffon custard

Chilled cucumber with seasoned cream *(Illustrated on page 55)*

METRIC/IMPERIAL	AMERICAN
20 cm/8 inch length cucumber	8 inch length cucumber
salt and pepper to taste	salt and pepper to taste
150 ml/¼ pint double cream	½ cup heavy cream
1 teaspoon lemon juice	1 teaspoon lemon juice
4 lettuce leaves	4 lettuce leaves
1 tablespoon drained capers	1 tablespoon drained capers

Peel the cucumber and slice very thinly. Spread the slices on a board, sprinkle with salt and allow to stand for 30 minutes. Drain well. Whip the cream with the lemon juice and season to taste. Arrange the lettuce leaves on 4 small plates, pile up the cucumber slices on the leaves and top with a swirl of seasoned cream. Scatter capers over the cream.

Andalusian chicken with olives ✱

METRIC/IMPERIAL	AMERICAN
25 g/1 oz butter	2 tablespoons butter
4 chicken portions	4 chicken portions
1 large onion	1 large onion
1 canned red pimento and 1 tablespoon liquid from can	1 canned red pimento and 1 tablespoon liquid from can
2 tablespoons oil	2 tablespoons oil
1 tablespoon flour	1 tablespoon flour
2 tablespoons tomato purée	2 tablespoons tomato paste
1 teaspoon sugar	1 teaspoon sugar
1 teaspoon dried oregano	1 teaspoon dried oregano
salt and pepper to taste	salt and pepper to taste
150 ml/¼ pint chicken stock	½ cup chicken broth
4 tablespoons dry sherry	4 tablespoons dry sherry
50 g/2 oz stuffed green olives	½ cup stuffed green olives
50 g/2 oz stoned black olives	½ cup pitted black olives

Put the butter in an ovenproof casserole and add the chicken skin side down. Cook in a moderately hot oven (190°C, 375°F, Gas Mark 5) for 20 minutes. Meanwhile prepare the sauce. Finely chop the onion and pimento. Heat the oil and use to fry the onion until limp but not brown. Stir in the flour until well blended then add the pimento and liquid, the tomato purée, sugar, oregano, salt and pepper to taste and cook over gentle heat for 2 minutes, stirring. Add the stock and sherry and continue cooking, stirring constantly, until the mixture forms a thick smooth sauce. Turn the chicken portions over, pour in the sauce, cover and return to the oven for a further 25 minutes, or until the chicken is tender. Stir in the olives, cover and keep hot. If frozen, add olives before reheating.

Gingered rice pilaff ✳

METRIC/IMPERIAL	AMERICAN
1 medium onion	*1 medium onion*
2 tablespoons oil	*2 tablespoons oil*
225 g/8 oz long grain rice	*generous 1 cup long grain rice*
600 ml/1 pint strong chicken stock	*2½ cups strong chicken broth*
1 teaspoon ground ginger	*1 teaspoon ground ginger*
salt and pepper to taste	*salt and pepper to taste*
1 tablespoon chopped parsley	*1 tablespoon chopped parsley*

Finely chop the onion. Heat the oil in a saucepan, add the onion and cook gently until transparent. Add the rice and cook over heat until just beginning to change colour. Add the stock, ginger and seasoning to taste, stir well and bring to the boil. Transfer to an ovenproof casserole dish, cover and cook in a moderately hot oven (190°C, 375°F, Gas Mark 5) for 45 minutes. Just before serving, fluff up lightly with a fork and sprinkle with the parsley. If frozen, reheat and garnish at serving time.

Torn spinach salad

Wash 10 fresh spinach leaves and shake dry. Remove stems, tear up the leaves and place in a salad bowl, together with 8 small sprigs of watercress. Make up a dressing with 1 tablespoon each of wine vinegar, orange juice and oil and season with a little salt and pepper. Just before serving, pour the dressing over the salad and toss lightly.

Peaches under a hazelnut crust ✳ *(Illustrated on page 58)*

METRIC/IMPERIAL	AMERICAN
6 ripe peaches	*6 ripe peaches*
50 g/2 oz soft brown sugar	*¼ cup light brown sugar*
¼ teaspoon ground cinnamon	*¼ teaspoon ground cinnamon*
200 g/7 oz plain flour	*1¾ cups all-purpose flour*
100 g/4 oz butter	*½ cup butter*
50 g/2 oz sugar	*¼ cup sugar*
50 g/2 oz chopped toasted hazelnuts	*½ cup chopped toasted hazelnuts or filberts*

Peel the peaches, halve them and remove the stones. Cut into thick slices and place in the base of an ovenproof dish or roaster. Mix together the brown sugar and cinnamon and sprinkle over the fruit. Sift the flour into a bowl and rub in the butter. Stir in most of the sugar and half the nuts. Spoon the mixture evenly over the peaches and scatter the remaining sugar and nuts over the top. Bake in a moderately hot oven (190°C, 375°F, Gas Mark 5) for 40–45 minutes. Serve with Chiffon custard.

Chiffon custard

METRIC/IMPERIAL	AMERICAN
2 eggs	*2 eggs*
50 g/2 oz castor sugar	*¼ cup granulated sugar*
300 ml/½ pint milk	*1¼ cups milk*

Whisk together the eggs and sugar. Heat the milk almost to boiling point then pour into the egg mixture, whisking well. Cook in a double boiler over simmering water, stirring all the time, until the custard coats the back of a spoon. Strain into a bowl and chill. Whisk with an electric mixer or rotary beater until foamy and serve in a small open jug.

Work plan for this menu

To prepare complete menu in 1½ hours ready to serve dinner at 8.15 pm.

Begin at:

6.30	Lay table
6.40	Make chiffon custard and chill
6.50	Prepare cucumber for starters
6.55	Prepare chicken and put in oven
7.00	Make sauce for chicken
7.10	Prepare pilaff and put in oven – chop parsley
7.20	Make spinach salad and prepare dressing
7.25	Turn chicken and add sauce
7.30	Prepare peaches under a hazelnut crust and put in oven
7.40	Whip cream and make cucumber starters; place on table.
7.45	Whisk chiffon custard
7.50	Check pilaff and chicken are ready, stir olives into chicken
7.55	Reduce oven heat to low. Turn off later when peaches are ready
8.00	Change ready to receive your guests.

Remember such details as having dressing ready to pour over salad at serving time, chopped parsley to sprinkle over pilaff.

Chapter 3
Weekends in style

Having people to stay over a whole weekend is quite a challenge. You want to look and be charming, enjoy the company of your guests, and make them feel it is a pleasure to entertain them. The house must be extra clean and tidy, family on best behaviour, and meals impeccable.

Some little thing frequently goes wrong, but most mistakes can be glossed over; the only exception being a total flop with the food. No-one will eat burnt toast or over-seasoned stew just out of politeness, and enjoy it! So your reputation as a cook is likely to rate higher than ever or drop disastrously after a weekend visit, because it is put to a considerable test. You have to produce not just one super meal, but perhaps as many as eight varied ones, one after the other, without much rest in between.

It is important to make a rough menu plan for the entire weekend, leaving it flexible on some points. The snack meal and main meal can often be reversed, if it turns out that your visitors prefer to eat more in the middle of the day than in the evening. A light meal can be fortified by serving soup as an extra course first, or ending with a cheeseboard. That is why I recommend freezing concentrated soups and unusual sauces. Either can be whisked out of freezer storage, quickly thawed, and with very little effort provide hearty nourishment in place of the iced tea and cucumber sandwiches you had planned to serve.

If not needed, frozen soups and sauces can comfortably await their call for months longer. Even frozen sandwiches, scheduled to be laid out decoratively on a plate to defrost for a couple of hours before teatime or to serve with coffee, can be transformed. Brush them with melted butter or oil, or dip them in egg and milk. Place in a buttered ovenproof dish, and bake until crunchy in a hot oven. Since salad ingredients and eggs do not freeze well, the fillings are likely to be those that heat, melt a little, and combine very temptingly; cheese is especially good.

It is annoying to discover that a guest dislikes some dish you have prepared as part of the plan. If you have no freezer and expect to bake tarts and flans while visitors are on the way to your home, do not make two flans exactly alike – for a party of six or more you will need two anyway. Omit shellfish from the savoury filling of one and put in diced salame instead, in case someone is coming who cannot see a shrimp without beginning to sniffle or break out in a rash. The same applies to strawberries; if you bake them in double crust pies or serve raw in tartlets, with a shiny glaze, use alternative fillings with some other berry fruit, for those who must shun strawberries!

And here is another golden hint. When you have chosen the food and halfway prepared it, do not ask guests 'what they would like' for any meal. Far better to tell them what is proposed, offer a choice if there is one, and enquire whether they will enjoy the menu. This gives them an opportunity to refuse some item politely. Only then, bring out your reserves. The same applies to drinks. Suggest three possibilities, and let guests choose without having to wonder wildly whether you can meet a demand for extremely dry sherry or a vodkatini.

Storecupboard starter

METRIC/IMPERIAL	AMERICAN
5 lettuce leaves, shredded	*5 lettuce leaves, shredded*
3 sticks celery, sliced	*3 stalks celery, sliced*
3 tablespoons mayonnaise	*3 tablespoons mayonnaise*
3 tablespoons tomato ketchup	*1 tablespoon tomato catsup*
½ teaspoon lemon juice	*½ teaspoon lemon juice*
225 g/8 oz shelled prawns	*½ lb shelled shrimp*
326 g/11½ oz can sweetcorn kernels	*11½ oz can corn kernels*
8 prawns in the shell	*8 shrimp in the shell*

Mix together the shredded lettuce and celery slices. Divide evenly between 4 small serving plates. Combine the mayonnaise, ketchup and lemon juice and stir in the shelled prawns. Pile the sweetcorn on the lettuce in the centre of the plates and surround with the shellfish mixture. Serve each starter garnished with 2 prawns in the shell.   *Serves 4.*

Calves' liver pâté ✱

METRIC/IMPERIAL	AMERICAN
450 g/1 lb calves' liver	*1 lb veal liver*
50 g/2 oz butter	*¼ cup butter*
100 g/4 oz belly of pork	*¼ lb belly of pork*
1 tablespoon chopped parsley	*1 tablespoon chopped parsley*
pinch of dried thyme	*dash of dried thyme*
1 clove of garlic, crushed	*1 clove of garlic, crushed*
1 tablespoon lemon juice	*1 tablespoon lemon juice*
1 egg	*1 egg*
salt and pepper to taste	*salt and pepper to taste*
100 g/4 oz chicken livers	*¼ lb chicken livers*
2 tablespoons brandy	*2 tablespoons brandy*
100 g/4 oz streaky bacon	*¼ lb bacon*

Cut the calves' liver into pieces and brown lightly in the butter, then mince finely with the pork. Add the parsley, thyme, crushed garlic, lemon juice and the beaten egg. Mix well and add salt and pepper to taste. Trim the chicken livers and fry in the remaining fat until just firm. Remove from the pan and slice. Add the brandy to the juices left in the pan, mix well and ignite. Stir into the liver mixture. Derind, then stretch the bacon with a palette knife and use to line an oval ovenproof dish. Half fill with the minced liver mixture, spread the chicken liver on top and cover with the remaining liver mixture. Fold the ends of the bacon over the top. Cover with lid or buttered foil and put into a roasting tin. Pour in cold water to come about 2·5 cm/1 in up the sides of dish. Cook in a moderate oven (170°C, 325°F, Gas Mark 3) for 2 hours. Cover with more buttered foil and weight the top. Leave until cold then turn out on a serving dish.   *Serves 6.* If frozen wrap in foil. Defrost in refrigerator to serve.

Pork terrine with herbs ✳

METRIC/IMPERIAL
225 g/8 oz leaf spinach
225 g/8 oz pork
75 g/3 oz cooked ham
1 small onion, chopped
1 clove garlic, crushed
1 tablespoon chopped basil
1 tablespoon chopped parsley
1½ teaspoons chopped chervil
pinch of dried rosemary
1 egg
pinch of cayenne pepper
pinch of ground nutmeg
3–4 thin strips pork fat
tomato wedges

AMERICAN
½ lb leaf spinach
½ lb pork
⅓ cup chopped cooked ham
1 small onion, chopped
1 clove garlic, crushed
1 tablespoon chopped basil
1 tablespoon chopped parsley
1½ teaspoons chopped chervil
dash of dried rosemary
1 egg
dash of cayenne pepper
dash of ground nutmeg
3–4 thin strips pork fat
tomato wedges

Cook the spinach in 2 tablespoons boiling salted water for 5 minutes. Drain, press out as much moisture as possible and chop roughly. Cut the pork into pieces and mince finely. Add the spinach and mince again. Dice the ham and add to the pork mixture with the onion, garlic, basil, parsley, chervil and rosemary. Stir in the beaten egg, cayenne and nutmeg, and salt and pepper to taste. Press the mixture into a lightly buttered oval ovenproof dish. Cover with strips of pork fat and cook in a moderate oven (170°C, 325°F, Gas Mark 3) for 1 hour. Serve cold, sliced and garnished with tomato wedges. *Serves 4*. If frozen, wrap in foil. Defrost in refrigerator. Garnish when serving.

Smooth chicken liver pâté ✳

METRIC/IMPERIAL
1 onion, chopped
25 g/1 oz butter
100 g/4 oz pig's liver
225 g/8 oz chicken livers
1 clove garlic, crushed
300 ml/½ pint chicken stock
2 tablespoons sherry
1 tablespoon lemon juice

AMERICAN
1 onion, chopped
2 tablespoons butter
¼ lb pork liver
8 oz chicken livers
1 clove garlic, crushed
1¼ cups chicken broth
2 tablespoons sherry
1 tablespoon lemon juice

Sauté the onion in the butter until softened. Slice the pig's liver and add to the pan with the chicken livers, crushed garlic and stock. Bring to the boil, cover and simmer for 1 hour. Allow to cool. Put half the mixture into a liquidizer and blend until really smooth. Turn into a basin and repeat with the remaining mixture. Mix in the sherry and lemon juice and add salt and pepper to taste. Spoon into a buttered ovenproof dish, cover with buttered foil and cook in a moderate oven (180°C, 350°F, Gas Mark 4) for 1½ hours. Remove from the oven, cover with more foil and weight the top. Cool, then chill before serving. *Serves 4–6*. If frozen, wrap in foil. Defrost in refrigerator. Garnish when serving.

Salame and mushroom flan *

METRIC/IMPERIAL
225 g/8 oz shortcrust pastry
1 medium onion, sliced
2 tablespoons oil
100 g/4 oz button mushrooms, sliced
225 g/8 oz salame, chopped
300 ml/½ pint milk
150 ml/¼ pint single cream
3 eggs
salt and pepper to taste
50 g/2 oz cheese, grated

AMERICAN
½ lb basic pastry
1 medium onion, sliced
2 tablespoons oil
1½ cups sliced button mushrooms
½ lb salame, chopped
1¼ cups milk
½ cup light cream
3 eggs
salt and pepper to taste
½ cup grated cheese

Roll out the pastry and use to line a shallow oval ovenproof dish. Prick the base and bake 'blind' in a moderately hot oven (190°C, 375°F, Gas Mark 5) for 5 minutes. Fry the onion gently in the oil for a few minutes. Add the mushrooms and fry until they start to soften. Mix the fried onion and mushroom with the chopped salame and spoon into the pastry case. Beat together the milk, cream, eggs and seasoning to taste. Pour into the flan case and sprinkle with the grated cheese. Bake at the same temperature for 40 minutes.   *Serves 6.* If frozen, cool and wrap in dish in foil. Reheat to serve.

Sausage wheel flan ✱

METRIC/IMPERIAL
100 g/4 oz shortcrust pastry
150 g/6 oz butter
1 small onion, chopped
100 g/4 oz cooked ham, chopped
100 g/4 oz mushrooms, sliced
1 tablespoon flour
300 ml/½ pint milk
salt, pepper, ground nutmeg to taste
1 egg yolk
2 tablespoons double cream
8 chipolata sausages
40 g/1½ oz cheese, grated

AMERICAN
¼ lb basic pastry
¾ cup butter
1 small onion, chopped
¼ lb cooked ham, chopped
¼ lb mushrooms, sliced
1 tablespoon flour
1¼ cups milk
salt, pepper, ground nutmeg to taste
1 egg yolk
2 tablespoons heavy cream
8 link sausages
⅓ cup grated cheese

Roll out the pastry thinly and use to line a 20 cm/8 in flan ring standing on an ovenproof plate. Bake blind in a moderately hot oven (190°C, 375°F, Gas Mark 5) for 10–15 minutes. Meanwhile, heat one-third of the butter and use to fry the onion, ham and mushroom until the onion is soft. Allow to cool. Melt half the remaining butter, stir in the flour. Gradually add the milk and bring to the boil, stirring constantly. Add salt, pepper and nutmeg to taste. Remove from the heat and stir in the egg yolk and cream. Fry the sausages in the remaining butter until golden brown. Put the onion, mushroom and ham mixture into the pastry case. Arrange the sausages on top like the spokes of a wheel. Pour the sauce over and sprinkle with the grated cheese. Bake in a moderately hot oven (200°C, 400°F, Gas Mark 6) for about 20 minutes. *Serves 4.* If frozen, cool and wrap on plate in foil. Reheat to serve.

Smoked mackerel pie ✱

METRIC/IMPERIAL
4 fillets smoked mackerel
2 medium onions, sliced
2 tablespoons chopped parsley
3 hard-boiled eggs, sliced
300 ml/½ pint single cream
3 tablespoons fresh white breadcrumbs
50 g/2 oz cheese, grated
cayenne pepper

AMERICAN
4 fillets smoked mackerel
2 medium onions, sliced
2 tablespoons chopped parsley
3 hard-boiled eggs, sliced
1¼ cups light cream
3 tablespoons fresh white breadcrumbs
½ cup grated cheese
cayenne pepper

Cut the fillets of smoked mackerel into strips. Mix the fish with the sliced onion, salt and pepper to taste, and the chopped parsley. Put half the mixture into a shallow oval ovenproof dish. Top with the sliced hard-boiled eggs, and then with the remaining fish mixture. Pour over the cream and sprinkle with the breadcrumbs and cheese. Bake in a moderately hot oven (190°C, 375°F, Gas Mark 5) for 30 minutes. Sprinkle with a little cayenne pepper before serving. *Serves 4.* If frozen, cool and wrap in dish in foil. Reheat and sprinkle with cayenne to serve.

Gnocchi ✳

METRIC/IMPERIAL	AMERICAN
600 ml/1 pint milk	*2½ cups milk*
1 onion	*1 onion*
1 bay leaf	*1 bay leaf*
5 tablespoons semolina	*5 tablespoons semolina flour*
100 g/4 oz cheese, grated	*1 cup grated cheese*
15 g/½ oz butter	*1 tablespoon butter*
1 teaspoon prepared mustard	*1 teaspoon prepared mustard*
salt and pepper to taste	*salt and pepper to taste*

Put the milk, onion and bay leaf into a saucepan and bring very slowly to the boil, so that the milk becomes well flavoured. Discard the flavourings and sprinkle on the semolina. Cook, stirring constantly for 15 minutes. Remove from the heat and stir in half the grated cheese, the butter, mustard and salt and pepper to taste. Spread the mixture in a flat tray to a depth of 2 cm/¾ in and cool. When quite cold cut into squares. Arrange the gnocchi in a shallow ovenproof dish, sprinkle with the remaining cheese and bake in a moderately hot oven (200°C, 400°F, Gas Mark 6) for 20 minutes, or until golden brown.   *Serves 4*. If frozen, sprinkle with cheese and reheat at serving time.

Peking plum chicken ✳

METRIC/IMPERIAL	AMERICAN
4 breast and wing chicken portions	*4 breast and wing chicken portions*
salt and pepper to taste	*salt and pepper to taste*
2 tablespoons oil	*2 tablespoons oil*
1 onion, chopped	*1 onion, chopped*
150 ml/¼ pint water	*½ cup of water*
2 teaspoons curry powder	*2 teaspoons curry powder*
1 tablespoon cornflour	*1 tablespoon cornstarch*
367 g/13 oz can pineapple pieces	*13 oz can pineapple pieces*
4 tablespoons plum jam	*4 tablespoons plum or other red jam*
1 oz flaked almonds	*2 tablespoons slivered almonds*

Lay the chicken portions in an oval ovenproof dish and season with salt and pepper. Heat the oil and use to fry the onion until transparent. Add the water and curry powder. Cover the pan and cook gently for 2 minutes. Blend the cornflour with 150 ml/¼ pint/⅔ cup of the pineapple syrup, stir into the pan and cook until thickened, stirring all the time. Blend in the plum jam until it is fully melted. Scatter the pineapple and almonds over the chicken and spoon over the sauce. Cover with a lid or foil and cook in a moderate oven (180°C, 350°F, Gas Mark 4) for 50 minutes, until tender. Serve with buttered noodles   *Serves 4*. If frozen, reheat covered. Cook noodles at serving time.
Note: Cooked chicken may be used for this dish, or if you require to defrost frozen chicken portions in a hurry, place them in the casserole, just cover with strong chicken stock (broth) and cook, uncovered, in a slightly hotter oven for 15 minutes, then drain before continuing as above.

Curried chicken avocados

METRIC/IMPERIAL
175 g/6 oz cooked chicken, chopped
4 tablespoons fresh white breadcrumbs
1 tablespoon mango chutney
2 teaspoons curry powder
1 medium onion, grated
salt and pepper to taste
150 ml/¼ pint soured cream
2 large ripe avocados
little lemon juice

AMERICAN
1 cup cooked chicken, chopped
4 tablespoons fresh white breadcrumbs
1 tablespoon mango chutney
2 teaspoons curry powder
1 medium onion, grated
salt and pepper to taste
½ cup soured cream
2 large ripe avocados
little lemon juice

Mix together chopped chicken with the breadcrumbs, mango chutney, curry powder, grated onion and salt and pepper to taste. Stir in 2 tablespoons of the soured cream. Cut the avocado pears in half and remove the stones. Brush the cut surfaces of the avocados with lemon juice and fill the hollows with the curried chicken mixture. Stand each filled half avocado in a small oatmeal bowl and spoon over the remaining soured cream. Bake in a moderately hot oven (190°C, 375°F, Gas Mark 5) for 20 minutes. Serve with a green salad and extra mango chutney. *Serves 4.*

Spicy cheesy chicken ✽

METRIC/IMPERIAL	AMERICAN
4 chicken portions	4 chicken portions
salt and pepper to taste	salt and pepper to taste
1 small green pepper	1 small green pepper
1 tablespoon oil	1 tablespoon oil
2 medium onions, sliced	2 medium onions, sliced
2 sticks celery, sliced	2 stalks celery, sliced
396 g/14 oz can tomatoes	14 oz can tomatoes
1 tablespoon prepared horseradish	1 tablespoon prepared horseradish
75 g/3 oz Edam cheese, grated	¾ cup grated Edam cheese

Place the chicken portions in a shallow ovenproof dish and season to taste. Bake in a moderately hot oven (200°C, 400°F, Gas Mark 6) for 30–40 minutes. Deseed and slice the green pepper. Heat the oil, add the prepared onion, celery and pepper and fry gently for about 10 minutes, or until soft. Add the tomatoes and their liquid, the horseradish and salt and pepper to taste. Stir well and pour over the chicken portions. Sprinkle with the grated cheese and return to the oven for a further 15 minutes.   *Serves 4.* If frozen, sprinkle with cheese and reheat at serving time.

Quick moussaka ✽

METRIC/IMPERIAL	AMERICAN
425 g/15 oz can minced beef in gravy	15 oz can ground beef in gravy
396 g/14 oz can tomatoes	14 oz can tomatoes
1 teaspoon sugar	1 teaspoon sugar
salt and pepper to taste	salt and pepper to taste
450 g/1 lb cold boiled potatoes, sliced	2 cups sliced cooked potatoes
25 g/1 oz butter	2 tablespoons butter
25 g/1 oz flour	¼ cup flour
300 ml/½ pint hot milk	1¼ cups hot milk
50 g/2 oz Cheddar cheese, grated	½ cup grated Cheddar cheese

Spread the canned beef in the bottom of a greased deep ovenproof dish. Drain and roughly chop the tomatoes and spoon over the meat. Season with the sugar and salt and pepper to taste. Top with sliced potatoes. Melt the butter in a saucepan, stir in the flour and cook, stirring, for 2 minutes. Gradually add the hot milk and bring to the boil, stirring constantly, until the sauce is thick and smooth. Remove from the heat, season to taste and add half the grated cheese. Pour over the potatoes, sprinkle with the remaining cheese and bake in a moderately hot oven (190°C, 375°C, Gas Mark 5) for 20–30 minutes.   *Serves 4.* If frozen, sprinkle with cheese and reheat at serving time.

Hebridean sausage loaf *

METRIC/IMPERIAL	AMERICAN
100 g/4 oz streaky bacon or bacon pieces	*¼ lb bacon or bacon pieces*
1 large onion	*1 large onion*
2 eggs	*2 eggs*
350 g/12 oz minced pork, veal or beef	*1½ cups ground pork, veal or beef*
1 teaspoon salt	*1 teaspoon salt*
½ teaspoon pepper	*½ teaspoon pepper*
½ teaspoon dry mustard	*½ teaspoon dry mustard*
1 teaspoon dried mixed herbs	*1 teaspoon dried mixed herbs*
75 g/3 oz quick cook oats	*1¼ cups quick cooking oats*
150 ml/¼ pint strong stock	*½ cup strong broth*
100 g/4 oz toasted breadcrumbs	*1 cup toasted breadcrumbs*

Derind the bacon then mince with the onion into a large mixing bowl. Beat the eggs and add to the bowl with the meat, salt, pepper, mustard, herbs, oats and stock. Mix thoroughly. Shape the mixture into a large sausage shape and wrap tightly in foil. Place in a shallow ovenproof dish and bake in a moderate oven (180°C, 350°F, Gas Mark 4) for 1 hour. Carefully remove the foil, and press the breadcrumbs all over the loaf. Slice the loaf and serve hot with vegetables or cold with a green salad.   *Serves 6.* If frozen, add breadcrumbs and reheat at serving time.

Tongue in wine sauce

METRIC/IMPERIAL	AMERICAN
25 g/1 oz butter	*2 tablespoons butter*
25 g/1 oz flour	*¼ cup flour*
½ teaspoon dry mustard	*½ teaspoon dry mustard*
425 g/15 oz can beef consommé	*15 oz can beef broth*
2 tablespoons red wine	*2 tablespoons red wine*
salt and pepper to taste	*salt and pepper to taste*
453 g/1 lb can ox tongue	*1 lb can beef tongue*
parsley sprigs	*parsley sprigs*

Melt the butter in a saucepan. Stir in the flour and mustard and cook gently for 3 minutes. Gradually add the beef consommé and red wine and bring to the boil, stirring constantly, until the sauce is smooth and thick. Remove from heat and season to taste. Slice the tongue neatly and arrange in a shallow ovenproof plate. Pour over the sauce and place in a moderate oven (170°C, 325°F, Gas Mark 3) for 15 minutes. Garnish with parsley sprigs before serving.   *Serves 4.*

Pineapple peach cobbler ✳

METRIC/IMPERIAL
225 g/8 oz flour
25 g/1 oz cornflour
½ teaspoon salt
175 g/6 oz butter
4 tablespoons water
filling:
225 g/8 oz sugar, 25 g/1 oz cornflour,
   50 g/2 oz butter, 450 ml/¾ pint pineapple
   juice, 4 peaches, 4 canned pineapple rings
   1 teaspoon lemon juice

AMERICAN
2 cups all-purpose flour
2 tablespoons cornstarch
½ teaspoon salt
¾ cup butter
4 tablespoons water

1 cup sugar, 2 tablespoons cornstarch,
   ¼ cup butter, scant 2 cups pineapple juice,
   4 peaches, 4 canned pineapple rings,
   1 teaspoon lemon juice

Sift the flour, cornflour and salt together into a bowl. Cut butter into pieces and add to the dry ingredients with the water. Mix well with a fork until the mixture forms a ball. Chill for 30 minutes. Roll out two-thirds of the pastry and use to line a shallow oven-proof dish. Bake 'blind' in a hot oven (220°C, 425°F, Gas Mark 7) for 10 minutes. Remove from the oven and allow to cool while you prepare the filling. Combine the sugar, cornflour and half the butter with the pineapple juice in a small pan. Stir briskly until boiling and cook for 5 minutes. Peel and slice the peaches and arrange in the pastry case. Cut the pineapple into pieces, and add to the peach slices. Sprinkle with the lemon juice. Pour the pineapple juice mixture over and dot with the remaining butter. Roll out the rest of the pastry and cut into strips. Arrange in a lattice pattern over the fruit. Cook in a cool oven (150°C, 300°F, Gas Mark 2) for about 30 minutes.   *Serves 4.*

Hot butterscotch sauce over rice ✳

METRIC/IMPERIAL
50 g/2 oz round grain rice
600 ml/1 pint milk
50 g/2 oz sugar
25 g/1 oz butter
75 g/3 oz soft brown sugar
200 ml/7 fl oz boiling water
4 teaspoons cornflour
25 ml/1 fl oz cold water
pinch of salt
¼ teaspoon vanilla essence

AMERICAN
¼ cup short grain rice
2½ cups milk
¼ cup sugar
2 tablespoons butter
⅓ cup light brown sugar
scant 1 cup boiling water
4 teaspoons cornstarch
2 tablespoons cold water
dash of salt
¼ teaspoon vanilla extract

Place the rice, milk and sugar in a saucepan. Bring slowly to the boil and stir well. Simmer for about 30 minutes until thick, stirring frequently. Meanwhile melt the butter and brown sugar gently together in a small saucepan. Stir in the boiling water. Moisten the cornflour with the cold water and stir into the hot mixture. Cook, stirring constantly, until thickened. Blend in the salt and vanilla essence. Turn the cooked rice into 4 oatmeal bowls. Pour over the sauce and bake in a moderately hot oven (190°C, 375°F, Gas Mark 5) for 20 minutes.   *Serves 4.*

| Weekend brunch menu for two people | Chilled apricot nectar
Egg and kipper croquettes
Eastern dream coffee |

(Illustrated on page 76)

This is an easy meal to serve as so much can be prepared in advance. If it is for brunch, add to the menu plenty of hot toast with butter and chunky marmalade. If it is for supper, serve a cheese board, and a bowl of polished apples.

Chilled apricot nectar

Mix together 100 ml/4 fl oz/½ cup canned or bottled apricot juice with 300 ml/½ pint/ 1½ cups fresh orange juice, 1 tablespoon apricot brandy and 1 teaspoon lemon juice. Stir well and serve poured over cracked ice in tulip-shaped wine glasses. *Serves 2 generously.*

Egg and kipper croquettes *

METRIC/IMPERIAL	AMERICAN
1 onion, chopped	*1 onion, chopped*
25 g/1 oz butter	*2 tablespoons butter*
450 ml/¾ pint thick savoury white sauce	*2 cups thick savory white sauce*
3 hard-boiled eggs, chopped	*3 hard-boiled eggs, chopped*
225 g/8 oz kipper fillets, flaked	*½ lb kipper fillets, flaked*
2 tablespoons chopped parlsey	*2 tablespoons chopped parsley*
1 egg, beaten	*1 egg, beaten*
dry breadcrumbs for coating	*dry breadcrumbs for coating*
oil for deep frying	*oil for deep frying*
4 tablespoons tartare sauce	*4 tablespoons tartare sauce*
lemon wedges	*lemon wedges*
parsley sprigs	*parsley sprigs*

Fry the onion gently in the butter until soft. Add to the white sauce with the chopped hard-boiled egg, flaked fish, chopped parsley and salt and pepper to taste. Divide the mixture into 8 equal portions and form each into a croquette shape. Dip in beaten egg and coat evenly in breadcrumbs. Repeat the coating process if necessary. Fry the croquettes in hot oil until crisp, golden brown and cooked through. Drain well on absorbent kitchen paper. Put the croquettes on to a shallow oval ovenproof dish. Spoon over the tartare sauce and glaze under a hot grill. Serve garnished with lemon wedges and parsley sprigs. *Serves 2 generously.* If frozen, reheat.

Eastern dream coffee

Pour 600 ml/1 pint/2½ cups boiling water over 4 tablespoons finely ground coffee in a warm jug. Add 1 teaspoon ground cardamon seeds, 1 tablespoon cold water and stir. Sweeten to taste. Allow to stand for 2 minutes and pour carefully through a fine strainer into stoneware goblets or large coffee cups. Half-whip 150 ml/¼ pint/½ cup whipping cream and float on top of the hot spiced coffee, reserving some for the 'second cups'.

Weekend outdoor buffet for eight people	*Egg and pineapple daisies* *Layered terrine of chicken with* *Hot rolls and butter* *Mexican plate pie* *Glazed apple flan* *Dandy fizz and iced lemon tea*

(Illustrated on page 75)

Egg and pineapple daisies

Drain 4 thin canned pineapple rings and marinate in 4 tablespoons French (Italian) dressing for about 1 hour. Half-fill 4 small dessert dishes with finely shredded Webb (Iceberg) lettuce. Drain the pineapple rings and place one on each dish. Pour the marinade over the lettuce. Shell 4 hard-boiled eggs and slice evenly with an egg slicer. Arrange the larger egg slices to make a circle on each pineapple ring, overlapping them slightly. Chop the white 'ends' off all the eggs. Place a spoonful of mayonnaise in the centre of each ring and top this with chopped egg white. Surround with capers to resemble the 'heart' of the daisy. Serve at once before the lettuce becomes limp.   *Serves 4 ; to serve 8, double the quantities.*

Layered terrine of chicken ✳

METRIC/IMPERIAL	AMERICAN
1 large mild onion	*1 large mild onion*
1 shallot or 2 spring onions	*1 shallot or 2 scallions*
1–1¼ kg/2–2½ lb chicken	*2–2½ lb chicken*
225 g/8 oz veal	*½ lb veal*
225 g/8 oz pork	*½ lb pork*
1 teaspoon chopped parsley	*1 teaspoon chopped parsley*
½ teaspoon ground allspice	*½ teaspoon ground allspice*
1 bay leaf	*1 bay leaf*
3 rashers bacon, derinded	*3 slices bacon, derinded*

Finely chop the onion and shallot. Skin the chicken, remove the breast and cut into thin slices. Remove all the rest of the flesh from the chicken and mince finely with the veal and pork. Add the onion, shallot, parsley and allspice. Mix well and add salt and pepper to taste. Butter an oval ovenproof dish, put in the bay leaf and rashers of bacon. Add alternate layers of meat mixture and slices of chicken until all is used up, ending with a layer of meat mixture. Cover and stand the dish in a roasting tin. Pour in cold water to come about 1 cm/½ in up sides of the dish. Cook in a moderate oven (170°C, 325°F, Gas mark 3) for 1½ hours. Cover with buttered foil and put a weight on top. Allow to get cold. Turn out on an oval platter and serve cut into slices. If the terrine is kept in the refrigerator still in the dish, pour a little melted pork fat over the surface.   *Serves 6–8.* If frozen, wrap in foil. Defrost in refrigerator to serve.

A weekend outdoor buffet for 8 : egg and pineapple daisies, layered terrine of chicken and mexican plate pie. In the background, glazed apple flan and dandy fizz.

Mexican plate pie *

METRIC/IMPERIAL
225 g/8 oz shortcrust pastry
½ green pepper
2 tablespoons oil
1 small onion, chopped
450 g/1 lb minced beef
salt and black pepper to taste
1–2 teaspoons mild chilli powder
250 ml/8 fl oz condensed tomato soup
6–8 stuffed green olives, sliced

AMERICAN
½ lb basic pastry
½ green pepper
2 tablespoons oil
1 small onion, chopped
1 lb ground beef
salt and black pepper to taste
1–2 teaspoons mild chili powder
1 cup condensed tomato soup
6–8 stuffed green olives, sliced

Roll out half the pastry and use to line a 25 cm/10 in ovenproof plate. Deseed and chop the green pepper. Heat the oil and use to fry the chopped onion and pepper gently until soft. Add the beef and cook until browned, stirring frequently. Add the salt, black pepper, chilli powder and tomato soup and bring to the boil. Simmer for 15 minutes. Allow to cool, then stir in the sliced olives. Spoon the mixture into the pastry case. Roll out the remaining pastry and cut into thin strips. Arrange over the meat in a closed lattice pattern. Bake in a moderately hot oven (200°C, 400°F, Gas Mark 6) for 30–40 minutes.   *Serves 4; to serve 8, make two plate pies.*

Glazed apple flan *

METRIC/IMPERIAL
75 g/3 oz butter
5 tablespoons sugar
175 g/6 oz plain flour
1 egg yolk
350 g/12 oz cooking apples
350 g/12 oz dessert apples
a little lemon juice
4 tablespoons apricot jam, warmed

AMERICAN
⅓ cup butter
5 tablespoons sugar
1½ cups all-purpose flour
1 egg yolk
¾ lb baking apples
¾ lb eating apples
a little lemon juice
4 tablespoons apricot jam, warmed

To make the pastry, cream the butter and 2 tablespoons of the sugar until soft and light. Add the flour and mix together. Stir in the egg yolk, and just enough water to bind. Chill while preparing the filling. Peel and core the cooking apples, chop them roughly, and cook with 2 tablespoons sugar to give a thick purée. Peel, core and thinly slice the rest of the apples and place in cold water to which a little lemon juice has been added. Roll out the pastry and use to line a 20 cm/8 in flan ring standing on an ovenproof plate. Bake 'blind' in a hot oven (220°C, 425°F, Gas Mark 7) for 10 minutes. Cool slightly, then spread with the apple purée. Cover with concentric circles of the apple slices and sprinkle with the remaining sugar. Return to a moderately hot oven (200°C, 400°F, Gas Mark 6) for about 15–20 minutes. Sieve the warm apricot jam and use to glaze the flan. Remove the flan ring and serve on the ovenproof plate.   *Serves 4; to serve 8, make two flans.* If frozen, chill and wrap on plate in foil. Serve cold.

A weekend lunch menu for two: chilled
apricot nectar, egg and kipper croquettes and
eastern dream coffee.

Dandy fizz

Strain 450 ml/¾ pint/4 cups chilled fresh orange juice into a stoneware jug. Add 8 table-spoons Grenadine (pomegranate juice) or strawberry syrup and stir well. When ready to serve, pour in 1 litre/1¾ pints/scant 5 cups semi-sparkling white wine. Serve in wine glasses before the sparkle subsides.   *Serves 4–6. If this is to be the only beverage, make double the quantity.*

Beef and mushroom plate pie ✳

METRIC/IMPERIAL	AMERICAN
225 g/8 oz shortcrust pastry	½ lb basic pastry
1 medium onion	1 medium onion
25 g/1 oz butter	2 tablespoons butter
1 tablespoon corn oil	1 tablespoon corn oil
100 g/4 oz mushrooms, sliced	¼ lb mushrooms, sliced
2 tablespoons flour	2 tablespoons flour
1 beef stock cube	1 beef bouillon cube
300 ml/½ pint water	1¼ cups water
350 g/12 oz cooked beef, chopped	1½ cups cooked chopped beef
2 teaspoons chopped parsley	2 teaspoons chopped parlsey
1 teaspoon prepared horseradish	1 teaspoon prepared horseradish
salt and pepper to taste	salt and pepper to taste
little milk	little milk

Roll out half the pastry and use to line a 20 cm/8 inch round ovenproof dish. Chop the onion finely. Heat the butter and oil in a pan, add onion and mushrooms and fry gently until the onion is beginning to colour. Stir in the flour and crumbled stock cube then gradually add the water and bring to the boil, stirring constantly. Cook for 3 minutes. Stir in the meat, parsley, horseradish, and salt and pepper to taste. Spoon the meat mixture into the pastry case. Roll out the remaining pastry and use to cover the pie. Dampen the edges and press well together. Brush the pie with a little milk and bake in a moderately hot oven (200°C, 400°F, Gas Mark 7) for 30–35 minutes.   *Serves 4–6. If frozen, reheat.*

Chapter 4
Snack suppers

Life has a different rhythm these days. The set meals of the past are often altered to accommodate our changing patterns of work and play. Sunday dinner at one, with a roast and deep-dish fruit pie, may give way to brunch at eleven; or the big family get-together of the week switched to Friday evening instead. Snack meals are indispensable to our new lifestyle.

More and more youngsters demand quick meals to fit into their school and social plans, and cannot be fed at the time which suits everyone else. They bring home friends quite casually, at any time of the day, and of course they are all starving for a delicious snack meal. Some of our traditional snacks are becoming costly, or do not fit into a diet (often a preoccupation of teenagers as much as of the housewife). Bacon and eggs? Always acceptable but weighted with calories, and certainly not a cheap filler for young people with hearty appetites. Try some of these original ideas for light meals. None outrageously expensive to produce, some to be eaten hot in winter, and others to team with summer salads. Indeed salads have become a year-round necessity to many, and quite a few are suggested elsewhere in this book. But here are extra ideas guaranteed to turn a small portion of savoury flan or supper dish into a balanced meal for dieters.

1. *College salad:* Buy a 225 g/8 oz bag of prepared mixed shredded salad vegetables, or make up your own by finely shredding a little white and red cabbage, some raw leek and carrot, and mix well together. This keeps well for up to a week in the refrigerator, in a closed polythene bag. At serving time, finely slice two small button mushrooms and a sprig of parsley for each person. Put in a salad bowl with 2 tablespoons fresh orange juice. Toss in the juice, add the shredded vegetables and toss again. Serve with shredded lettuce or alone. For non-dieters, whisk 1 teaspoon of oil into the orange juice. Serve seasoned if required, but it is better not to season it.

2. *Zippy cottage cheese:* Combine 225 g/8 oz low-calorie cottage cheese with 1 small can of anchovies, finely chopped, and 1 small pickled cucumber finely sliced. Use a little of the oil from the can, a little brine from the cucumber jar, and 1 teaspoon lemon juice to make a dressing. Put scoops of the cheese salad into lettuce leaf cups, and spoon over the dressing for non-dieters, or seasoning only for dieters. Cottage cheese is the mainstay of many diet meals, and fortunately it takes well to many flavours.

3. *Tomates à la française:* Put six medium tomatoes in a heatproof bowl or jug, pour over sufficient boiling water to cover. Allow to stand one minute, drain off the water, and slip off the tomato skins. Slice finely on to a flat plate. Chop together 2 trimmed spring onions and 2 sprigs each of parsley and mint. Add either capers or shredded celery to the mixture. Sprinkle over the salad. Serve *au naturel* without any dressing. Cover and chill slightly first if possible.

Kipper and potato bake

METRIC/IMPERIAL	AMERICAN
450 g/1 lb potatoes	*1 lb potatoes*
225 g/8 oz kipper fillets	*½ lb kipper fillets*
1 medium onion, grated	*1 medium onion, grated*
2 tablespoons chopped parsley	*2 tablespoons chopped parlsey*
2 eggs	*2 eggs*
300 ml/½ pint milk	*1¼ cups milk*
150 ml/¼ pint single cream	*½ cup light cream*
salt and pepper to taste	*salt and pepper to taste*
50 g/2 oz butter	*¼ cup butter*

Slice the potatoes thinly. Flake the kipper fillets, removing any skin and bones. Grease a shallow oval or square ovenproof dish and arrange the sliced potato, kipper and onion in alternate layers, sprinkling parsley between each, finishing with a layer of potato. Beat together the eggs, milk and cream with seasoning to taste. Pour over the potato and kipper and dot the surface with pieces of butter. Bake in a moderately hot oven (190°C, 375°F, Gas Mark 5) for 45 minutes.   *Serves 6.*

Prawn and rice casserole

METRIC/IMPERIAL	AMERICAN
4 rashers bacon	*4 slices bacon*
1 small onion, chopped	*1 small onion, chopped*
225 g/8 oz long grain rice	*1 generous cup long grain rice*
396 g/14 oz can tomatoes	*14 oz can tomatoes*
300 ml/½ pint water	*1¼ cups water*
1 bay leaf	*1 bay leaf*
salt and pepper to taste	*salt and pepper to taste*
225 g/8 oz shelled prawns or scampi	*2 cups shelled shrimp, or jumbo shrimp*

Derind and dice the bacon. Fry it slowly until crisp. Remove from the pan with a slotted draining spoon. Add the chopped onion and rice to the bacon fat in the pan and stir over low heat for about 5 minutes, until the onion is soft and the rice transparent. Transfer to a medium ovenproof casserole and add the tomatoes and their liquid, the water, bay leaf and seasoning to taste. Cover and cook in a cool oven (150°C, 300°F, Gas Mark 2) for about 30 minutes. Add the bacon pieces and shellfish. Stir in gently and return to the oven for a further 10 minutes.   *Serves 4.*

Potato and smoked haddock soufflé

METRIC/IMPERIAL	AMERICAN
450 g/1 lb potatoes	*1 lb potatoes*
25 g/1 oz butter	*2 tablespoons butter*
2 tablespoons milk	*2 tablespoons milk*
salt and pepper	*salt and pepper*
225 g/8 oz cooked smoked	*½ lb cooked finnan haddie,*
haddock, flaked	*flaked*
grated zest of ½ lemon	*grated rind of ½ lemon*
2 tablespoons chopped parsley	*2 tablespoons chopped parsley*
150 ml/¼ pint double cream	*½ cup heavy cream*
3 eggs, separated	*3 eggs, separated*
2 hard-boiled eggs, chopped	*2 hard-boiled eggs, chopped*

Cook the potatoes in boiling water until just tender. Drain well and mash with the butter, milk and seasoning to taste. Add the flaked fish, grated lemon zest, chopped parsley, cream, egg yolks and chopped hard-boiled egg. Whisk the egg whites until stiff and fold gently into the potato and fish mixture. Spoon into a greased medium ovenproof casserole. Bake in a moderately hot oven (190°C, 375°F, Gas Mark 5) for 45 minutes. *Serves 6.*

Potato and cheese sausage soufflés

METRIC/IMPERIAL	AMERICAN
350 g/12 oz soft mashed potato	*1½ cups soft mashed potato*
175 g/6 oz grated cheese	*1½ cups grated cheese*
4 sausages, skinned	*4 large link sausages, skinned*
salt and pepper to taste	*salt and pepper to taste*
2 tablespoons chopped parsley	*2 tablespoons chopped parsley*
25 g/1 oz butter, melted	*2 tablespoons melted butter*
4 eggs, separated	*4 eggs, separated*
1 small onion, sliced	*1 small onion, sliced*

Beat the mashed potato with two-thirds of the grated cheese. Slice the skinned sausages, and add to the potato mixture with seasoning to taste, the parsley, melted butter and egg yolks. Beat well. Whisk the egg whites until stiff and fold in lightly. Divide the mixture among 4 greased deep individual ovenproof dishes. Divide the onion slices into rings, and place a few on top of each soufflé. Sprinkle with the remaining cheese, and bake in a moderately hot oven (190°C, 375°F, Gas Mark 5) for 35–40 minutes, until well risen and pale golden. *Serves 4.*

Spinach and pasta mornay

METRIC/IMPERIAL	AMERICAN
225 g/8 oz noodles	*½ lb noodles*
40 g/1½ oz butter	*3 tablespoons butter*
40 g/1½ oz flour	*⅓ cup flour*
450 ml/¾ pint milk	*2 cups milk*
150 ml/¼ pint double cream	*½ cup heavy cream*
salt and pepper to taste	*salt and pepper to taste*
100 g/4 oz cheese, grated	*1 cup grated cheese*
225 g/8 oz cooked chopped spinach	*1 cup cooked chopped spinach*
4 eggs	*4 eggs*
paprika	*paprika*

Cook the noodles in a large pan of boiling salted water until just tender. Drain well. To make the cheese sauce, melt the butter in a pan, stir in the flour and cook for 1 minute. Gradually add the milk and bring to the boil, stirring constantly until thickened. Stir in the cream, seasoning, and three-quarters of the grated cheese. Mix the cooked noodles with half the cheese sauce. Put half the noodle mixture into a greased dish. Top with the spinach, then cover with the rest of the noodle mixture. Make 4 dimples in the top and drop an egg into each one. Spoon over the remaining cheese sauce. Scatter over the rest of the cheese. Bake in a moderately hot oven (190°C, 375°F, Gas Mark 5) for 30 minutes. Sprinkle with paprika before serving.   *Serves 4.*

Curried lasagne *

METRIC/IMPERIAL
1 onion, chopped
2 tablespoons oil
225 g/8 oz minced beef
1 tablespoon curry powder
396 g/14 oz can tomatoes
300 ml/½ pint beef stock
1 tablespoon tomato purée
salt and pepper to taste
175 g/6 oz lasagne
2 tablespoons grated
  or desiccated coconut
50 g/2 oz cheese, grated
fried onion rings

AMERICAN
1 onion, chopped
2 tablespoons oil
½ lb ground beef
1 tablespoon curry powder
14 oz can tomatoes
1¼ cups beef broth
1 tablespoon tomato paste
salt and pepper to taste
6 oz lasagne noodles
2 tablespoons shredded
  coconut
½ cup grated cheese
fried onion rings

Fry the onion gently in the oil for a few minutes. Add the minced beef and cook, stirring, until browned. Stir in the curry powder and cook for 1 minute. Add the canned tomatoes and their liquid, the stock, tomato purée and seasoning to taste. Bring to the boil and simmer for 20 minutes. Put a layer of the sauce into the base of a greased medium oven-proof casserole and top with a layer of *dry* lasagne. Repeat with alternating layers of sauce and lasagne, finishing with a layer of sauce. Sprinkle the top with the grated coconut and cheese. Bake in a moderate oven (180°C, 350°F, Gas Mark 4) for 45 minutes. Garnish with rings before serving.   *Serves 6*. If frozen, add onion rings and reheat at serving time.

Cheese and sausage pudding

METRIC/IMPERIAL
450 g/1 lb beef sausages, cooked
2 large onions, sliced
butter
4 slices bread, toasted
3 eggs
450 ml/¾ pint milk
salt and pepper to taste
75 g/3 oz cheese, grated
1 tablespoon chopped parsley

AMERICAN
1 lb beef link sausages, cooked
2 large onions, sliced
butter
4 slices bread, toasted
3 eggs
2 cups milk
salt and pepper to taste
¾ cup grated cheese
1 tablespoon chopped parsley

Cut each sausage into slices, lengthways. Fry the sliced onions gently in 25 g/1 oz/2 tablespoons butter until soft and pale golden. Spread the toasted bread with butter and cut into triangles. Arrange the sausages, onions and bread in layers in a greased oval ovenproof dish. Beat the eggs with the milk, seasoning and grated cheese. Pour the cheese custard over the layered ingredients and leave to stand for 30 minutes. Bake in a moderately hot oven (190°C, 375°F, Gas Mark 5) for 40 minutes. Serve sprinkled with chopped parsley.   *Serves 6*.

French onion pancakes *(Illustrated on page 93)*

METRIC/IMPERIAL	AMERICAN
100 g/4 oz plain flour	1 cup all-purpose flour
1 teaspoon dry mustard	1 teaspoon dry mustard
salt and pepper to taste	salt and pepper to taste
1 egg	1 egg
150 ml/¼ pint milk	½ cup milk
150 ml/¼ pint brown ale	¾ cup beer
oil	oil
2 large onions, sliced	2 large onions, sliced
50 g/2 oz butter	¼ cup butter
326 g/11½ oz can sweetcorn kernels	11½ oz can corn kernels
300 ml/½ pint savoury white sauce	1¼ cups savory white sauce
100 g/4 oz cheese, grated	1 cup grated cheese
2 rashers bacon, grilled	2 slices bacon, broiled

Sift the flour with the dry mustard and seasoning to taste. Add the egg and half the milk and beat to a smooth batter. Gradually beat in the remaining milk and the brown ale. Leave the batter to stand for 1 hour. Lightly oil an omelette pan and use the batter to make 8 pancakes. Stack them on a plate and keep warm. Fry the sliced onions in the butter until soft and pale golden. Divide the fried onions among the pancakes and roll up. Put the sweetcorn into a shallow oval ovenproof dish and place the filled pancakes on top. Mix the sauce with half the cheese and spoon over the pancakes. Sprinkle with the remaining cheese. Bake in a moderately hot oven (190°C, 375°F, Gas Mark 5) for 30 minutes. Crumble the bacon and sprinkle over the pancakes before serving.   *Serves 4.* If frozen, add bacon and reheat at serving time.

Glazed parsnip bake with ham

METRIC/IMPERIAL	AMERICAN
1 kg/2 lb parsnips, halved	2 lb parsnips, halved
2 tablespoons corn oil	2 tablespoons corn oil
100 g/4 oz soft brown sugar	½ cup light brown sugar
grated zest and juice of 1 large lemon	grated rind and juice of 1 large lemon
2 tablespoons orange jelly marmalade	2 tablespoons orange jelly marmalade

Quarter any parsnips which are large and pare away the central core. Parboil in lightly salted water for 5 minutes, or until just beginning to soften. Drain well and transfer to a greased shallow ovenproof dish. Place the oil, brown sugar, lemon juice and zest in a saucepan and bring slowly to the boil, stirring until the sugar dissolves. Simmer for 2 minutes, then stir in the marmalade until melted. Pour the glaze over the parsnips and bake in a moderately hot oven (190°C, 375°F, Gas Mark 5) for 15 minutes. Remove the dish from the oven, turn the parsnips and baste well. Return to the oven for a further 10 minutes, or until the parsnips are tender. Serve with ham.   *Serves 4–6.*

Ratatouille pancakes ✳

METRIC/IMPERIAL
3 tablespoons oil
1 small onion, sliced
1 aubergine, chopped
3 courgettes, sliced
4 tomatoes, sliced
1 tablespoon tomato purée
salt and pepper to taste
1 clove of garlic, crushed
8 small pancakes, as previous recipe
300 ml/½ pint savoury white sauce
100 g/4 oz cheese, grated

AMERICAN
3 tablespoons oil
1 small onion, sliced
1 eggplant, chopped
3 zucchini, sliced
4 tomatoes, sliced
1 tablespoon tomato paste
salt and pepper to taste
1 clove of garlic, crushed
8 small pancakes, as previous recipe
1¼ cups savory white sauce
¾ cup grated cheese

Heat the oil and use to fry the sliced onion gently for 5 minutes. Add the chopped aubergine, sliced courgette and tomato, and cook gently until the vegetables soften. Add the tomato purée, seasoning and garlic, and simmer for a further 10 minutes. Divide the filling between the pancakes and roll them up. Arrange the filled pancakes in a greased oval ovenproof dish. Mix the white sauce with half the grated cheese and bake in a moderately hot oven (190°C, 375°F, Gas Mark 5) for 30 minutes. Sprinkle with the rest of the cheese. *Serves 4.* If frozen, sprinkle with cheese and reheat at serving time.

Saucy layered marrow

METRIC/IMPERIAL
1 small vegetable marrow
50 g/2 oz butter
2 tablespoons finely chopped fresh mixed
  herbs (mint, tarragon, parsley)
salt and pepper to taste
300 ml/½ pint thick cheese sauce
25 g/1 oz fresh breadcrumbs
50 g/2 oz cheese, grated

AMERICAN
1 acorn squash
¼ cup butter
2 tablespoons finely chopped fresh mixed
  herbs (mint, tarragon, parsley)
salt and pepper to taste
1¼ cups thick cheese sauce
½ cup fresh breadcrumbs
½ cup grated cheese

Peel the marrow, cut into rings and remove the pith and seeds. Cut each ring into 4. Parboil in a little salted water for 5 minutes. Drain, add the butter and toss the marrow pieces to coat them evenly. Place a layer of marrow in a buttered shallow oval ovenproof dish and sprinkle with the herbs and seasoning to taste. Spoon over some of the sauce. Make 2 more layers of marrow and sauce in the same way, sprinkling each layer with herbs and seasoning and ending with a layer of sauce. Sprinkle with the breadcrumbs and grated cheese and bake in a moderately hot oven (200°C, 400°F, Gas Mark 6) for 20 minutes. *Serves 4.*

Devilled drumsticks *

METRIC/IMPERIAL	AMERICAN
8 chicken drumsticks	8 chicken drumsticks
3 tablespoons oil	3 tablespoons oil
6 spring onions, chopped	6 scallions, chopped
1 tablespoon vinegar	1 tablespoon vinegar
½ teaspoon Tabasco sauce	½ teaspoon Tabasco sauce
1 teaspoon Worcestershire sauce	1 teaspoon Worcestershire sauce
1 tablespoon tomato ketchup	1 tablespoon tomato catsup

Brush the drumsticks with oil and arrange close together in a shallow ovenproof dish or roaster. Bake in a moderately hot oven (200°C, 400°F, Gas Mark 6) for 15 minutes. Turn the drumsticks over and cook for a further 10 minutes. Meanwhile, heat the remaining oil and use to fry the chopped onions gently until soft. Add the remaining ingredients and bring to the boil, stirring constantly. Taste and adjust the seasoning if necessary. Spoon the sauce over the drumsticks and return to the oven for a further 5 minutes. Serve with plain oven-baked rice (See page 61 for method).   *Serves 4.* If frozen, reheat covered. Cook rice at serving time.

Cheese-baked potatoes

METRIC/IMPERIAL	AMERICAN
225 g/8 oz onions	½ lb onions
50 g/2 oz butter	¼ cup butter
¾ kg/1¾ lb potatoes	1¾ lb potatoes
100 g/4 oz Gruyère cheese	¼ lb Swiss cheese
250 ml/8 fl oz chicken stock	1 cup chicken broth
few drops of Worcestershire sauce	few drops of Worcestershire sauce
¼ teaspoon ground nutmeg	¼ teaspoon ground nutmeg
salt and pepper to taste	salt and pepper to taste

Thinly slice the onions. Melt the butter and use to fry the onion gently until soft. Thinly slice the potatoes and the cheese. Layer the onion, potato and cheese together in a small ovenproof casserole. Pour in the stock, Worcestershire sauce and nutmeg and season to taste. Cover and cook in a moderately hot oven (190°C, 375°F, Gas Mark 5) for 1 hour. *Serves 4–6.*

Baked beans with pineapple

Snip up 4 rashers derinded bacon and place in a frying pan. Cook gently over moderate heat to render out as much of the fat as possible. Add the contents of 2 425 g/15 oz/ 1 lb cans of baked beans and a 379 g/13½ oz can of crushed pineapple including the syrup. Stir over moderate heat until well blended. Taste and adjust the seasoning. If liked, include 1 teaspoon prepared mustard. Dip 4 large slices white bread quickly in water just to moisten (if the bread is soaked too much the fat may splutter). Fry the bread slices in a mixture of bacon dripping and butter until golden brown on both sides. Place each slice on a small ovenproof plate and spoon over the baked bean mixture. Put the plates on a baking sheet and place in a moderate oven (180°C, 350°F, Gas Mark 4) for 15 minutes to heat through.

Variations:

1. Combine chopped canned mandarin oranges and 6 tablespoons of the syrup with the beans instead of the pineapple.
2. Fry 225 g/8 oz/2 cups diced cucumber in butter and stir in 6 tablespoons stock. Add to the beans instead of the pineapple.
3. To make a more substantial meal, dip the bread slices into a mixture made by beating up 1 egg in 100 ml/4 fl oz/½ cup milk, instead of the water.

Bacon and apple supper

METRIC/IMPERIAL
225 g/8 oz streaky bacon
little prepared mustard
3 large cooking apples, peeled
100 g/4 oz butter
225 g/8 oz fine fresh white breadcrumbs
225 g/8 oz Samsoe or Cheddar cheese, grated
salt and pepper to taste
sprigs of parsley

AMERICAN
½ lb bacon
little prepared mustard
3 large baking apples, pared
½ cup butter
4 cups fine fresh white breadcrumbs
2 cups grated Danish or Cheddar cheese, grated
salt and pepper to taste
sprigs of parsley

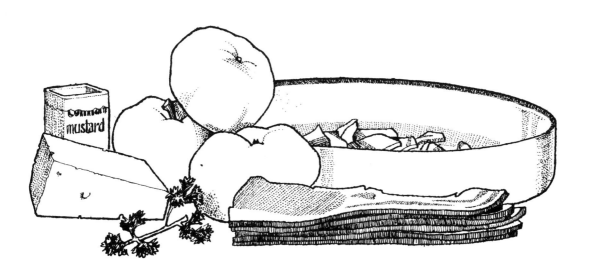

Derind all the bacon rashers and reserve 4 for the topping. Roughly chop the remainder and place in a shallow oval ovenproof dish. Spread with a little mustard. Core and grate the apples. Melt the butter and stir in the breadcrumbs, grated apple, three-quarters of the grated cheese and seasoning to taste. Spread this mixture over the bacon and mustard in the dish, sprinkle with the remaining cheese and top with the reserved bacon. Bake in a moderate oven (180°C, 350°F, Gas Mark 4) for 45 minutes. Garnish with parsley sprigs and serve hot with tomato ketchup (catsup). *Serves 4.*

Cheese and tomato meringue

METRIC/IMPERIAL	AMERICAN
75 g/3 oz Samsoe cheese, grated	¾ cup grated Danish cheese
2 eggs, separated	2 eggs, separated
salt and pepper to taste	salt and pepper to taste
butter	butter
2 thick slices of bread, trimmed	2 thick slices of bread, trimmed
2 tomatoes, sliced	2 tomatoes, sliced

Mix the grated cheese and egg yolks together, and season well with salt and pepper to taste. Butter the bread slices, and place them buttered side down in a shallow ovenproof dish so that the buttered side will become crisp. Arrange the tomato slices round the edge of the bread slices, and divide the cheese mixture between them. Whisk the egg whites until stiff and pile on top of the cheese mixture. Bake in a moderately hot oven (200°C, 400°F, Gas Mark 6) for 20–25 minutes. Serve immediately.   *Serves 2.*

Aubergine pizza * *(Illustrated on page 94)*

METRIC/IMPERIAL	AMERICAN
225 g/8 oz plain flour	2 cups all-purpose flour
salt and pepper to taste	salt and pepper to taste
15 g/½ oz fresh yeast	1 tablespoon fresh yeast
about 150 ml/¼ pint tepid water	about ½ cup tepid water
1 aubergine, sliced	1 eggplant, sliced
oil	oil
1 onion, finely chopped	1 onion, finely chopped
225 g/8 oz tomatoes, chopped	½ lb tomatoes, chopped
1 tablespoon tomato purée	1 tablespoon tomato paste
1 clove of garlic, crushed	1 clove of garlic, crushed
1 teaspoon dried oregano	1 teaspoon dried oregano
75 g/3 oz Mozzarella cheese, sliced	3 oz Mozzarella cheese, sliced

Sift the flour and 1 teaspoon of salt into a bowl. Rub in the yeast and add sufficient tepid water to make an elastic dough. Put the dough into a floured bowl. Cover and leave in a warm place for 1 hour, or until doubled in size. To make the topping, put the aubergine into a colander and sprinkle generously with salt. Leave to drain for 30 minutes. Fry the onion until soft in 2 tablespoons of oil for 5 minutes. Add the tomatoes, tomato purée, garlic, oregano and seasoning to taste. Cook gently until thick and pulpy. Fry the aubergine slices on both sides in oil until pale golden. Knead the dough well and work in 2 tablespoons of oil. Press into a flat shape to fit a large ovenproof dinner plate. Brush the surface with oil, then spoon over the tomato sauce. Top with the aubergine slices and Mozzarella cheese. Sprinkle with a little oil and bake in a moderately hot oven (200°C, 400°F, Gas Mark 6) for 30 minutes. *Serves 6–8.* If frozen, cool and wrap in foil. Reheat on plate.

Boston pizza ✳

METRIC/IMPERIAL
basic pizza dough made with 225 g/8 oz
  flour (see page 88)
oil
425 g/15 oz can baked beans
225 g/8 oz chipolata sausages
6 rashers streaky bacon
salt and pepper to taste
50 g/2 oz cheese, grated

AMERICAN
basic pizza dough made with 2 cups flour
  (see page 88)
oil
1 lb can baked beans
½ lb small pork link sausages
6 slices streaky bacon
salt and pepper to taste
½ cup grated cheese

Make up the pizza dough and allow to rise for 1 hour, then knead in 2 tablespoons of oil. Press into a flat shape to fit a large ovenproof dinner plate. Brush the surface with oil. Spread the baked beans evenly over the dough, and arrange the sausages on top. Form a lattice with the bacon, and season to taste. Sprinkle with the grated cheese and a little oil. Bake in a moderately hot oven (200°C, 400°F, Gas Mark 6) for 30 minutes. *Serves 6–8*. If frozen, cool and wrap in foil. Reheat on plate.

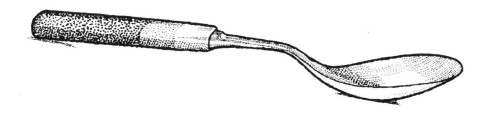

Cheese and walnut farls ✳

METRIC/IMPERIAL
225 g/8 oz self raising flour

50 g/2 oz butter
75 g/3 oz grated Samsoe cheese
pinch of salt
½ teaspoon dry mustard
2 tablespoons chopped walnuts
1 egg
150 ml/¼ pint milk

AMERICAN
2 cups all-purpose flour, sifted with 2
  teaspoons baking powder
¼ cup butter
¾ cup grated Danish cheese
dash of salt
½ teaspoon dry mustard
2 tablespoons chopped walnuts
1 egg
generous ½ cup milk

Sift the flour into a bowl and rub in the butter. Add the cheese, salt, mustard and nuts to the flour. Beat the egg and milk together and combine with the dry ingredients. Turn the mixture out on to a well greased 25 cm/10 inch ovenproof dinner plate, and cut almost through into quarters. Bake in a moderate oven (180°C, 350°F, Gas Mark 4) for 35–40 minutes.   *Serves 4*. If frozen, cool and wrap in foil. Reheat on plate.

Rich fruit supper scone ✳ *(Illustrated on page 37)*

METRIC/IMPERIAL	AMERICAN
225 g/8 oz self raising flour	2 cups all-purpose flour sifted with 2 teaspoons baking powder
75 g/3 oz butter	⅓ cup butter
50 g/2 oz sugar	¼ cup sugar
25 g/1 oz dried fruit (raisins or sultanas)	3 tablespoons dried fruit (seedless raisins or golden raisins)
1 egg	1 egg
little milk	little milk

Sift the flour into a bowl and rub in the butter. Stir in the sugar and dried fruit. Beat the egg and stir into the flour mixture until it forms a dough. It may be necessary to add a little milk but do not make the mixture too soft. Form the dough into a ball, place in the centre of a greased ovenproof plate and press gently to form a round which is raised slightly in the centre. Divide into six triangles with a knife, cutting to about half the depth of the scone. Brush with milk and bake in a moderately hot oven (200°C, 400°F, Gas Mark 6) for 25–30 minutes or until golden brown and firm to the touch. Serve very fresh.   *Serves 6*. If frozen, freeze uncooked. Bake from frozen for 10 extra minutes and complete recipe at serving time.

Rich tea scone: Omit the dried fruit and serve the scone with strawberry jam and thick cream.

Savoury scone: Omit the dried fruit and sugar and substitute ½ teaspoon dry mustard and salt and pepper to taste.

Apple cake ✳

METRIC/IMPERIAL	AMERICAN
200 g/8 oz self raising flour	2 cups all-purpose flour sifted with 2 teaspoons baking powder
100 g/4 oz butter	½ cup butter
100 g/4 oz sugar	½ cup sugar
450 g/1 lb cooking apples	1 lb baking apples
about 3 tablespoons milk	about 3 tablespoons milk

Sift the flour into a bowl and rub in the butter. Stir in the sugar. Peel, core and slice the apples and stir into the flour mixture. Add just sufficient milk to bind the mixture together and form into a ball with the fingertips. Place in the centre of a greased ovenproof plate and pat out gently to form a circle. Brush with milk and bake in a moderate oven (180°C, 350°F, Gas Mark 4) for 25–30 minutes. Serve hot or cold, with brown sugar and cream.   *Serves 4–6*. If frozen, cool and wrap in foil. Reheat on plate.

Chapter 5
Super sweets

The old-fashioned 'sweet tooth' may find no favour with dentists, or with doctors, but most of us still possess it. Somehow bowls full of fresh fruit do not always take the place of sweet puddings and desserts, and a really creamy rice pudding is just as much a treat to many as it was a hundred years ago, to our great-grand-parents.

None of the sweet dishes given in this book are excessively high in calories, or over-sugary, but if the recipes work just as well and please as much when made with less sugar, that is an advantage to the whole family. Sweetening, like seasoning, is very much a matter of personal taste, and those who like it and can afford the calories, will find it easy to add a sprinkling of extra sugar to their own portions. Cream is a pleasant extra with most desserts, but it can be made to go much further by half-whipping, then folding in a stiffly whisked egg white. Incidentally, egg white is far lower in calories than egg yolk, so there is hardly any increase in the fattening effect of cream lightened and extended in this way, and everyone can take a gorgeously satifying portion.

If there is some member of the family who is forbidden such goodies entirely, do not let him or her feel deprived while the others are joyously digging into a succulent sweet. Halve a really juicy ripe orange, scoop out the half segments into a footed desert dish, and squeeze in any remaining juice. Slice up half a banana into the dish and stir well to combine. At the expense of only 100 calories, this makes a delightful diet dessert.

Citrus sponge fool   ✳

METRIC/IMPERIAL
24 boudoir biscuits, halved
orange curaçao
3 oranges, 1 grapefruit
75 g/3 oz castor sugar
600 ml/1 pint double cream

AMERICAN
24 ladyfingers, halved
orange curaçao
3 oranges, 1 grapefruit
⅓ cup granulated sugar
2½ cups heavy cream

Dip the halved sponge fingers into orange curaçao and arrange 8 halves round the sides of each of 6 wine glasses. Grate the zest from 2 of the oranges. Squeeze the juice from the 3 oranges and the grapefruit. Mix the fruit juices and grated zest with the castor sugar. Whip the cream until quite thick and fold in the sweetened fruit juice mixture. Spoon into the prepared wine glasses and chill for at least 4 hours. The tops can be decorated with crystallized orange and lemon slices, if liked. *Serves 6*. If frozen, freeze in small dishes. Serve while still chilled.

Hot baked trifle

METRIC/IMPERIAL	AMERICAN
4 trifle sponges	4 small soft sponge cakes
lemon curd	lemon flavored spread or jam
150 ml/¼ pint sweet white wine	¾ cup sweet white wine
2 bananas	2 bananas
2 oranges	2 oranges
300 ml/½ pint milk	1¼ cups milk
150 ml/¼ pint single cream	½ cup light cream
3 eggs	3 eggs
50 g/2 oz castor sugar	¼ cup granulated sugar
50 g/2 oz flaked almonds	½ cup slivered almonds

Split the sponges and sandwich them together with lemon curd. Arrange in the base of a deep ovenproof dish and spoon over the white wine. Allow to stand for 30 minutes. Slice the bananas. Remove all the peel and pith from the oranges and cut the flesh into segments. Arrange the banana and orange over the soaked sponge. Whisk the milk, cream, eggs and sugar together and strain over the sponge and fruit. Stand the dish in a roasting tin and add sufficient water to the tin to come halfway up the sides of the dish. Bake in a moderate oven (180°C, 350°F, Gas Mark 4) for 30 minutes. Sprinkle with the nuts and return to the oven for a further 15 minutes.   *Serves 6.*

French onion pancakes and steamed peach soufflé.

Jam sandwich pudding

METRIC/IMPERIAL	AMERICAN
4 thin slices bread, well buttered	*4 thin slices bread, well buttered*
4 tablespoons raspberry jam	*4 tablespoons raspberry jam*
1 teaspoon grated lemon zest	*1 teaspoon grated lemon rind*
2 eggs	*2 eggs*
1 tablespoon sugar	*1 tablespoon sugar*
450 ml/¾ pint milk	*2 cups milk*

Butter a small deep ovenproof dish. Cut the slices of bread and butter into quarters. Line the bottom of the dish with half the bread, butter side down. Spread the jam over the bread in the dish and sprinkle with the lemon zest. Cover with the remaining bread, butter side up. Beat the eggs and sugar together. Stir in the milk and pour over the bread. Allow to stand for 20 minutes. Bake in a moderate oven (180°C, 350°F, Gas Mark 4) for 20 minutes, or until the top is crisp and golden brown.   *Serves 4–6.*

Chocolate sauce pudding ✳

METRIC/IMPERIAL	AMERICAN
75 g/3 oz plain flour	*¾ cup all-purpose flour*
2 tablespoons cocoa powder	*2 tablespoons unsweetened cocoa powder*
pinch of salt	*dash of salt*
100 g/4 oz butter	*½ cup butter*
100 g/4 oz sugar	*½ cup sugar*
2 eggs	*2 eggs*
½ teaspoon vanilla essence	*½ teaspoon vanilla extract*
1 tablespoon chopped walnuts	*1 tablespoon chopped walnuts*
1–2 tablespoons milk	*1–2 tablespoons milk*
sauce:	
100 g/4 oz soft brown sugar	*½ cup light brown sugar*
2 tablespoons cocoa powder	*2 tablespoons unsweetened cocoa powder*
300 ml/½ pint hot water	*1¼ cups hot water*

Sift the flour, cocoa and salt together. Cream the butter and sugar together until light and fluffy. Beat the eggs, add the vanilla essence and gradually beat into the creamed mixture alternately with the flour and cocoa. Add the walnuts and sufficient milk to make a fairly soft consistency. Place in a buttered deep ovenproof dish and spread evenly. To make the sauce, put the cocoa and sugar together in a basin, gradually add the hot water and mix until smooth. Pour the sauce on top of the pudding mixture and bake in a moderately hot oven (190°C, 375°F, Gas Mark 5) for about 40 minutes. During baking the sauce will drop to the bottom of the dish leaving the pudding mixture on top.   *Serves 4.* If frozen, reheat.

Aubergine pizza, chestnut cheesecake and orange caramel custards.

Chocolate and ginger date pudding ✳ *(Illustrated on page 36)*

METRIC/IMPERIAL
175 g/6 oz soft margarine
175 g/6 oz soft brown sugar
3 eggs
150 g/5 oz self raising flour
2 tablespoons cocoa powder
2 teaspoons baking powder
1½ teaspoons ground ginger
75 g/3 oz chopped stoned dates
4 tablespoons golden syrup
2 tablespoons lemon juice
1 tablespoon chopped preserved ginger

AMERICAN
¾ cup soft margarine
¾ cup light brown sugar
3 eggs
1¼ cups all-purpose flour
2 tablespoons unsweetened cocoa powder
3 teaspoons baking powder
1½ teaspoons ground ginger
½ cup chopped pitted dates
4 tablespoons light corn syrup
2 tablespoons lemon juice
1 tablespoon chopped preserved ginger

Put the margarine, brown sugar, eggs, flour, cocoa powder, baking powder and ground ginger into a bowl. Beat thoroughly for 3 minutes until smooth. Stir in the chopped dates and spoon into a greased shallow ovenproof dish. Bake in a moderate oven (180°C, 350°F, Gas Mark 4) for 1 hour, until firm to the touch. Meanwhile, heat the syrup with the lemon juice and chopped ginger but do not allow to boil. Stir well, spoon over the pudding as soon as it is removed from the oven, and serve immediately.   *Serves 6*. If frozen, cool, wrap in dish in foil. Make sauce, pour over and reheat at serving time.

Fluffy noodle pudding

METRIC/IMPERIAL
600 ml/1 pint milk
pinch of salt
225 g/8 oz broad noodles
50 g/2 oz butter
75 g/3 oz soft brown sugar
2 eggs, separated
1 teaspoon vanilla essence
50 g/2 oz walnuts, chopped
50 g/2 oz glacé cherries

AMERICAN
2½ cups milk
dash of salt
½ lb broad noodles
¼ cup butter
⅓ cup light brown sugar
2 eggs, separated
1 teaspoon vanilla extract
⅓ cup chopped walnuts
⅓ cup chopped candied cherries

Bring the milk and salt to the boil. Add the noodles and return to the boil. Cook until tender, stirring gently to keep the noodles separate. Soften the butter in a large bowl, beat in the sugar, and then the egg yolks. Gradually add the cooked noodles and the milk in which they were cooked, stirring all the time. Flavour with the vanilla essence. Whisk the egg whites until stiff and fold into the noodle mixture, scattering in the nuts and cherries to distribute them evenly. Turn into a buttered oval ovenproof dish and cover loosely with foil. Bake in a moderate oven (180°C, 350°F, Gas Mark 4) for 40–45 minutes, or until well risen and firm to the touch. Serve hot or cold with a compôte of fruit. *Serves 4*.

Steamed peach soufflé *(Illustrated on page 93)*

METRIC/IMPERIAL
420 g/15 oz can peach halves, drained
3 tablespoons cornflour
juice of ½ lemon
2 tablespoons castor sugar
4 eggs, separated
50 g/2 oz sponge cake crumbs
3 tablespoons peach brandy

AMERICAN
15 oz can peach halves, drained
3 tablespoons cornstarch
juice of ½ lemon
2 tablespoons granulated sugar
4 eggs, separated
4 tablespoons crumbled ladyfingers
3 tablespoons peach brandy

Blend the canned peaches to a purée in a liquidizer. Put the peach purée into a pan with the cornflour, lemon juice and castor sugar. Stir until smooth. Bring to the boil, stirring continuously until thickened. Allow to cool slightly. Beat in the egg yolks and the sponge cake crumbs. Whisk the egg whites until they form soft peaks and fold gently into the peach mixture. Put into a small buttered ovenproof casserole. Cover and place in a roasting tin. Pour in cold water to come 2·5 cm/1 in up the sides of the dish and cook in a moderately hot oven (190°C, 375°F, Gas Mark 5) for about 1 hour until well risen. Spoon the peach brandy over the cooked soufflé and serve immediately. *Serves 6.*

Gooseberry clafouti

METRIC/IMPERIAL
225 g/8 oz ripe dessert gooseberries
50 g/2 oz butter, diced
2 eggs
75 g/3 oz castor sugar
40 g/1½ oz flour
150 ml/¼ pint single cream
300 ml/½ pint milk
grated zest of 1 lemon
50 g/2 oz soft brown sugar

AMERICAN
½ lb ripe gooseberries
¼ cup butter, diced
2 eggs
⅓ cup granulated sugar
⅓ cup flour
½ cup light cream
1¼ cups milk
grated rind of 1 lemon
¼ cup light brown sugar

Top and tail the gooseberries. Put them into a shallow ovenproof dish with the butter. Heat through in a moderately hot oven (190°C, 375°F, Gas Mark 5) for 5 minutes. Meanwhile, make the batter. Whisk the eggs and castor sugar together in a basin. Whisk in the flour, then gradually whisk in the cream, milk, and lemon zest. Sprinkle the hot gooseberries with the brown sugar and pour over the lemon batter. Return to the oven and bake for 35 minutes. The clafouti can be eaten either hot or cold, with cream. It is much more solid when served cold. *Serves 6.* If frozen, defrost in refrigerator before reheating to serve.

Apple crunch pudding ✳

METRIC/IMPERIAL
1 kg/2 lb cooking apples
100 g/4 oz sugar
75 g/3 oz soft brown sugar
75 g/3 oz butter
2 tablespoons golden syrup
75 g/3 oz rolled oats

AMERICAN
2 lb baking apples
½ cup sugar
⅓ cup light brown sugar
⅓ cup butter
2 tablespoons light corn syrup
scant 1 cup uncooked quick cooking oats

Peel, core and slice the apples and arrange in a deep ovenproof dish with the sugar. Put the brown sugar, butter and golden syrup into a saucepan and heat gently, stirring, until the sugar has dissolved. Stir the oats into the butter and sugar mixture and spread over the apples, pressing down gently with the back of a spoon. Bake in a moderately hot oven (190°C, 375°F, Gas Mark 5) for 20–30 minutes, or until golden brown on top. *Serves 4–6*. If frozen, reheat.

Pineapple and soured cream crumble ✳

METRIC/IMPERIAL
1 medium size fresh pineapple
50 g/2 oz sugar
150 ml/¼ pint soured cream
175 g/6 oz self raising flour

75 g/3 oz butter
50 g/2 oz demerara sugar
grated zest of ½ orange
50 g/2 oz chopped hazelnuts

AMERICAN
1 medium size fresh pineapple
¼ cup sugar
½ cup soured cream
*1½ cups all-purpose flour sifted with 1½
teaspoons baking powder*
⅓ cup butter
¼ cup light brown sugar
grated rind of ½ orange
⅓ cup chopped hazelnuts

Remove the pine and outer peel from the pineapple. Chop the flesh, discarding any tough centre core. Mix the chopped pineapple with the sugar and soured cream and place in a greased oval ovenproof dish. Sift the flour and rub in the butter. Add the brown sugar, orange zest and chopped nuts and sprinkle over the pineapple mixture. Bake in a moderately hot oven (190°C, 375°F, Gas Mark 5) for 40 minutes. Serve with the simple pineapple sauce below.   *Serves 6*.

Pineapple Sauce: Place 225 g/8 oz/1 cup pineapple jam in a saucepan with 250 ml/ 8 fl oz/1 cup orange juice. Stir over a moderate heat until well blended.

Normandy apple meringue

METRIC/IMPERIAL
300 ml/½ pint cider
75 g/3 oz granulated sugar
small piece of cinnamon stick
thinly pared rind of ½ lemon
4 dessert apples
50 g/2 oz sultanas
2 egg whites
100 g/4 oz castor sugar
25 g/1 oz chopped nuts

AMERICAN
1¼ cups cider
⅓ cup sugar
small piece of cinnamon stick
thinly pared rind of ½ lemon
4 eating apples
4 tablespoons golden raisins
2 egg whites
½ cup granulated sugar
2 tablespoons chopped nuts

Put the cider and granulated sugar into a pan and stir over gentle heat until the sugar has dissolved. Add the cinnamon stick and lemon rind and simmer for 10 minutes. Take out the flavouring and discard. Peel, core and quarter the apples and add to the cider syrup. Poach gently for 5 minutes. Put the cooked apple, 3 tablespoons of the syrup and the sultanas into a shallow ovenproof dish. Whisk the egg whites until stiff. Add half the castor sugar and whisk again until stiff and glossy. Fold in the remaining sugar. Peak the meringue over the apples and sprinkle with the chopped nuts. Bake in a moderately hot oven (190°C, 375°F, Gas Mark 5) for 40 minutes. *Serves 4.*

Note: If liked, use up the remaining cider syrup to make a sauce. Boil to reduce by half, cool slightly, and whisk in 150 ml/¼ pint/½ cup single (light) cream.

Flambéed fruit compôte ✱

METRIC/IMPERIAL
6 small seedless oranges
6 canned pineapple rings
4 tablespoons apricot jam
grated zest and juice of 1 lemon
½ teaspoon ground cinnamon
100 g/4 oz soft brown sugar
50 g/2 oz unsalted butter
4 tablespoons white rum or brandy

AMERICAN
6 small seedless oranges
6 canned pineapple rings
4 tablespoons apricot jam
grated rind and juice of 1 lemon
½ teaspoon ground cinnamon
½ cup light brown sugar
¼ cup unsalted butter
4 tablespoons white rum or brandy

Pare off the zest of the oranges, and cut into very thin shreds. Remove all peel and pith from the oranges, but keep them whole. Place the oranges and pineapple rings in an ovenproof casserole and scatter over the orange zest. Heat together the jam, lemon zest and juice, cinnamon, sugar and butter. Stir well and pour over the fruit. Cover and cook in a moderately hot oven (200°C, 400°F, Gas Mark 6) for about 20 minutes. Just before serving, warm the rum or brandy in a ladle, ignite and pour over the fruit compôte. *Serves 6.* If frozen, cool, transfer to container, reheat in dish and flambé.

Alaska pancakes

METRIC/IMPERIAL	AMERICAN
8 thin pancakes	*8 thin pancakes*
396 g/14 oz can cherry pie filling	*14 oz can cherry pie filling*
8 scoops raspberry ripple ice cream	*8 scoops raspberry ripple ice cream*
3 egg whites	*3 egg whites*
175 g/6 oz castor sugar	*¾ cup granulated sugar*
2 tablespoons chopped nuts	*2 tablespoons chopped nuts*

Spread each pancake generously with cherry pie filling, reserving a little for the topping. Fold each pancake, envelope-fashion, around a scoop of raspberry ripple ice cream. Put the filled and folded pancakes into a shallow oval ovenproof dish and keep as cold as possible while you make the meringue. Whisk the egg whites until stiff. Add half the castor sugar and continue whisking until stiff. Fold in the remaining castor sugar. Spread the remaining cherry pie filling over the pancakes, and completely cover with peaks of meringue. Sprinkle with chopped nuts and bake in a hot oven (220°C, 425°F, Gas Mark 7) for about 8 minutes, until the peaks of the meringue are brown. Do not overcook otherwise the ice cream will be too soft. Serve immediately.   *Serves 4.*

Coffee crème brûlée

METRIC/IMPERIAL	AMERICAN
3 eggs	*3 eggs*
75 g/3 oz castor sugar	*⅓ cup granulated sugar*
1 tablespoon instant coffee	*1 tablespoon instant coffee*
450 ml/¾ pint single cream	*2 cups light cream*
few drops of almond essence	*few drops of almond extract*
50 g/2 oz chopped walnuts	*⅓ cup chopped walnuts*
demerara sugar	*light brown sugar*

Whisk the eggs with the castor sugar, instant coffee, cream and almond essence. Pour into a shallow ovenproof dish. Stand the dish in a roasting tin and add sufficient water to come halfway up the sides of the dish. Bake in a moderate oven (180°C, 350°F, Gas Mark 4) for 45 minutes. Remove from the oven and allow the custard to cool. Sprinkle with the nuts and a generous layer of demerara sugar. Put under a hot grill until the sugar turns golden brown and caramelizes. Allow to cool and then chill well before serving.   *Serves 6.*

Variations

Chocolate crème brûlée: Omit the coffee. Instead, mix 2 teaspoons cocoa powder with 1 tablespoon boiling water until smooth, and blend with the cream before whisking into the eggs.

Vanilla crème brûlée: Omit the coffee. Increase the almond essence to 1 teaspoon. Substitute toasted flaked almonds for the walnuts.

Fruit sherbet ✳

METRIC/IMPERIAL
225 g/8 oz granulated sugar
450 ml/¾ pint water
2 teaspoons gelatine
50 ml/2 fl oz cold water
*250 ml/8 fl oz fruit juice or 100 g/4 oz
    crushed fruit*
¼ teaspoon salt
2 tablespoons lemon juice
2 egg whites

AMERICAN
1 cup sugar
2 cups water
2 teaspoons unflavored gelatine
¼ cup cold water
1 cup fruit juice or ½ cup crushed fruit

¼ teaspoon salt
2 tablespoons lemon juice
2 egg whites

Mix the sugar and water in a saucepan and bring to the boil. Soften the gelatine in the cold water. Stir the softened gelatine into the boiling sugar syrup. Remove from the heat and allow to cool. Stir in the fruit juice or crushed fruit, the salt and lemon juice. Pack in shallow containers and freeze until mushy. Scoop into a chilled bowl and add the unbeaten egg whites. Beat with an electric mixer until light and fluffy. Pile the mixture up in 6 footed dessert dishes and freeze until firm. Cover the dishes with foil. Uncover and allow to soften at room temperature for 10 minutes before serving. *Serves 6.*

Note: The mixture can be frozen in a polythene container and scooped out into the dishes at serving time.

Chestnut cheesecake ✱
(Illustrated on page 94)

METRIC/IMPERIAL	AMERICAN
225 g/8 oz shortcrust pastry	½ lb basic pastry
225 g/8 oz cream cheese	8 oz package cream cheese
100 g/4 oz castor sugar	½ cup granulated sugar
3 eggs, separated	3 eggs, separated
175 g/6 oz unsweetened chestnut purée	⅔ cup unsweetened chestnut purée
300 ml/½ pint double cream	1¼ cups heavy cream

Put a large flan ring on a 25 cm/10 in ovenproof plate. Roll out the pastry and use to line the flan ring. Cream the cheese with the castor sugar. Beat in the egg yolks and the chestnut purée. Lightly whip the cream and stiffly whisk the egg whites. Fold the cream and egg whites into the creamed mixture. Spoon the cheesecake filling into the pastry case and smooth the top. Bake in a moderate oven (180°C, 350°F, Gas Mark 4) for about 1 hour, until the filling is firm but spongy to the touch. Allow to cool slightly, then remove the flan ring. Serve warm or cold with whipped cream. *Serves 8*. If frozen, wrap in foil, defrost in refrigerator to use.

Orange caramel custards ✱
(Illustrated on page 94)

METRIC/IMPERIAL	AMERICAN
4 eggs	4 eggs
75 g/3 oz castor sugar	⅓ cup granulated sugar
grated zest and juice of 1 orange	grated rind and juice of 1 orange
300 ml/½ pint milk	1¼ cups milk
300 ml/½ pint single cream	1¼ cups light cream
100 g/4 oz granulated sugar	½ cup sugar

Whisk the eggs with the castor sugar, grated orange zest, milk and cream. Strain the mixture into 6 covered soup bowls. Stand these in a roasting tin and add sufficient water to come halfway up the sides of the dishes. Put on the lids and bake in a moderate oven (180°C, 350°F, Gas Mark 4) for 45 minutes. Remove from the oven and allow to cool. Dissolve the granulated sugar in the orange juice in a small pan over gentle heat. Bring to the boil and simmer until the syrup begins to caramelize and just turns golden. Remove the pan from the heat and spoon a little of the caramel over the top of each orange custard. Allow to become quite cold before serving. *Serves 6*. If frozen, freeze uncooked, bake from frozen for 10 extra minutes and complete recipe at serving time.

Chapter 6
Microwave meals in minutes

Now that the microwave oven has been fully adapted to the domestic market, it has many attractive advantages for the busy housewife. Not too heavy to be moved easily from one site in the kitchen to another, it requires only a normal plug and socket such as you would use for a food mixer; and it is rapidly becoming reasonable in price.

Safe and simple

The safety features incorporated in all the new microwave ovens protect you from any possibility of misuse. The only important difference between this and conventional oven cooking is that metal containers (even china with a metallic decoration) often cannot be used at all. Foil dishes of course fall into this category but a small strip of thin foil can be wrapped round the bony portion of a joint or the ends of chicken legs or wings to protect them from over-cooking. However, this restriction is more than made up for by the variety of other utensils you can use for cooking which would not stand oven heat.

Because microwaves cook by disturbing the molecular structure of food, causing friction and therefore heat, the cooking utensil does not become hot at all, except through contact with the food itself as it cooks. You can use folded kitchen paper, waxed paper plates, china or glass dishes, even those that are not specially toughened (the latter would only be suitable for heating, not cooking). High-quality polythene containers, boiling bags and stoneware are ideal. Casseroles made of cast iron may have a brightly enamelled surface but being made of metal should not be used. Be sure to remove the twist tie if it has a metal thread in the centre before cooking or re-heating food in a bag, leaving the top lightly twisted together.

Quick defrosting

A microwave oven will certainly speed up defrosting, save washing up, and give you freedom to decide on a meal from the freezer a very short time before you require to cook it. Providing it is frozen in a suitable container such as stoneware, frozen food can go into the microwave, defrost in minutes, and reheat without damage to the container, while you lay the table and prepare a salad.

Microwave ovens vary in their capacity to cook a given quantity of food at one time. With practice you can discover whether it is speedier to partly cook one dish, remove it from the oven, and cook another dish while the first one 'rests' to carry on cooking in residual heat.

Time-saving tips

1. Dense foods such as a vegetable purée or baked beans should always be cooked first because they retain heat while other food is cooking. Heat them covered and set the timer for half the required time; remove the cover, stir well to speed heating and continue cooking for the rest of the necessary time. Naturally you will leave the lid in place and keep the dish warm while other items are being micro-cooked.

2.   It is frequently useful if food can be served out on to individual plates and one or more reserved to be reheated when a member of the family comes home late. For the best results, arrange the food to cover the plate in a thin layer rather than piling it all up in the centre. As the microwaves affect the food round the edge of the dish first, put dense items like meat and mashed potatoes round the outside and foods which heat quickly, like peas or a macédoine of vegetables, in the centre. Gravy or sauce should be spooned over the meat to prevent it from drying out.

3.   Reheating cooked food is often difficult to time. The best way to test it is by removing the plate from the oven and feeling underneath the plate in the centre. As soon as the food is hot enough in the centre to warm the plate it is ready to serve.

4.   The embargo on using metal in the microwave does not extend to silicone coated baking aids, but since the cooking process is considerably slowed down, you may decide not to use them either. In any event, none of these metal pieces should be allowed to touch the oven walls. If you are uncertain about the suitability of any material, place the empty dish in the oven for 30 seconds. If the dish becomes warm it should not be used, if only lukewarm it is suitable for heating but not cooking, and if it remains cool you can cook in it.

5.   Many microwave recipes call for the dish to be covered. To cover, use an inverted plate, several thicknesses of folded kitchen paper or a sheet of strong polythene.

6.   The rising of bread rolls can be much accelerated with this oven. Knead the dough then cover with wet kitchen paper and rise in the microwave for 15 seconds. Leave for 5 minutes. Repeat until double in bulk. Knock back, shape into fancy rolls and prove in the microwave. Cover again with wet paper, heat for 30 seconds and stand for 4 minutes. Repeat 3 times or until doubled in size. You can make yeasted bread, roll dough, rise, prove and bake all within an hour. If you use a bread mix, the whole process is even quicker.

7.   To melt a jelly (package of flavoured gelatin crystals), place it in a jug with 3 tablespoons water and cook for 30 seconds.

8.   To melt squares of chocolate or marshmallows, place in a bowl or jug, cook for 1 minute, then stir. Repeat if necessary.

9.   To micro-bake potatoes for a family meal, scrub, prick and bake them first for 5 to 10 minutes, or until potatoes feel slightly soft to pressure. Remove, wrap individually in foil; they will then continue to cook in residual heat and will remain hot for at least 20 minutes while you cook the other items on the menu.

10.   To micro-cook frozen vegetables quickly, place them while still frozen in a serving dish. Place small dots of butter round the edge of the dish and one in the centre, cover tightly with cling wrap and cook for 2 minutes. Shake dish, return to oven for a further 2 minutes. Vegetables such as peas will be cooked but larger vegetables may need a further 2 minutes. Be careful when removing the cover because steam will immediately escape, or puncture the top first.

11.   Dense foods which require to be stirred to heat or cook evenly, should always be stirred from the outside of the dish to the centre. Poultry or meat items cooked by the roasting method should be turned over once or twice during cooking. Small cuts should be turned over and repositioned to bring the part nearest the centre to the outside.

12.   To make instant coffee, tea from a tea bag or cocoa, the liquid can be heated to boiling point in the serving cup or mug in less time than it would take to boil a kettle. The handle of the cup remains cool.

Canadian chowder ✱

METRIC/IMPERIAL	AMERICAN
100 g/4 oz sliced bacon or salt pork, derinded	*¼ lb sliced bacon or salt pork, derinded*
2 large potatoes, diced	*2 large potatoes, diced*
1 medium onion, chopped	*1 medium onion, chopped*
450 g/1 lb smoked cod or coley, skinned	*1 lb smoked cod or finnan haddie, skinned*
2 tablespoons flour	*2 tablespoons flour*
450 ml/¾ pint milk	*2 cups milk*
salt and pepper to taste	*salt and pepper to taste*
150 ml/¼ pint single cream	*generous ½ cup light cream*

Finely chop the bacon or pork, place in a medium ovenproof casserole and cook for 2 minutes. Stir in the potato and onion, cover and cook for 4 minutes. Stir well, cover again and cook for a further 3–4 minutes, until the vegetables are tender. Cut the fish into bite-sized pieces and add to the casserole. Carefully stir in the flour, pour in the milk and stir gently. Cover and cook for 6 minutes. Season to taste and add the cream. Return the casserole to the oven, uncovered, and cook for 3 minutes, or until really hot. *Serves 4–6.*

Devilled party dip

Beat together 200 ml/6 fl oz/¾ cup evaporated milk with 225 g/8 oz/½ lb strong (sharp) Cheddar cheese, grated, 1 tablespoon prepared mustard and ½ teaspoon chilli sauce in a bowl. Cook for 3 minutes, stir well and return to the oven for a further 3 minutes. Remove and stir in 1 finely chopped canned pimento. Serve as a hot dip for fruit and vegetable 'dippers': surround the bowl of dip on a large platter with an assortment of apple wedges, orange segments, cauliflower florets, cucumber sticks, carrot spears, etc.

<table>
<tr><td>Menu</td><td>*Cosy cabbage with pork or lamb chops*
Micro-baked potatoes
Apricot crisp
Coffee</td></tr>
</table>

Cosy cabbage with pork or lamb chops

METRIC/IMPERIAL

1 medium firm white or red cabbage
1 large onion, chopped
2 tablespoons soft brown sugar
1 teaspoon caraway seeds (optional)
4 lean pork or lamb chump chops
4 thick rings of peeled apple
salt and pepper to taste
290 g/10¾ oz can condensed cream of
  mushroom or asparagus soup

AMERICAN

1 medium firm white or red cabbage
1 large onion, chopped
2 tablespoons light brown sugar
1 teaspoon caraway seeds (optional)
4 lean pork or sirloin of lamb chops
4 thick rings of pared apple
salt and pepper to taste
10¾ oz can condensed cream of mushroom
  or asparagus soup

Core and finely shred the cabbage. Mix with the onion, brown sugar and caraway seeds (if used) and place in a shallow ovenproof dish. Embed the chops in the cabbage, with the fat sides towards the edges of the dish. Core and place an apple ring on each chop and season to taste. Spoon the soup evenly over the dish. Do not cover as the dish will form a golden brown topping as it cooks. Place in the microwave and cook for 10 minutes. Give the dish a quarter turn and cook for a further 10 minutes. Test the chops with a fork to make sure they are tender. Cover the dish and allow to stand for a few minutes before serving.   *Serves 4.*

Apricot crisp

METRIC/IMPERIAL

396 g/14 oz can apricot pie filling
1 tablespoon sugar
grated zest and juice of 2 oranges
50 g/2 oz soft margarine
65 g/2½ oz rolled oats
75 g/2 oz soft brown sugar
3 tablespoons flour
4 ginger biscuits, crushed

AMERICAN

14 oz can apricot pie filling
1 tablespoon sugar
grated rind and juice of 2 oranges
¼ cup soft margarine
¾ cup uncooked quick cooking oats
⅓ cup light brown sugar
3 tablespoons flour
4 gingersnaps, crushed

Mix together the apricot pie filling, sugar, orange zest (rind) and juice in a shallow ovenproof dish. Combine the margarine, oats, brown sugar and flour, until crumbly. Spoon evenly over the fruit mixture and sprinkle with the biscuit crumbs. Place in the microwave and cook for about 10 minutes, or until fruit juices begin to bubble through the crisp crust. Serve warm with whipped cream.   *Serves 4.*

Chapter 7
How your freezer can help

A freezer is an invaluable piece of equipment to help you enjoy a busy and interesting life without having difficulty in coping with family meals as well as entertaining. If properly exploited, and not used merely as extra storage space for commercially frozen foods, the freezer has many useful possibilities. Of course you can limit shopping expeditions and still have on hand a good supply of all the foods you normally use. By buying these in bulk you are almost bound to save money. The best saving is in having storage space for your own cooked dishes, made during hours convenient to yourself and definitely economizing more in time and effort than just by oven cooking alone.

Saving time and trouble

It has been calculated that preparing a casserole dish with an assortment of ingredients takes a housewife 10–12 minutes before the cooking begins. But it only takes half as long again to treble the quantities and produce three separate meals. Clearing up afterwards takes virtually no longer. By using containers, bags or sheet wrapping which are moisture-vapour-proof (and manufacturers usually indicate clearly if their product is suitable for use in the freezer) you can store most made-up dishes without loss of quality for 4–6 months and raw or blanched fresh food for up to one year.

To make the best possible use of precious oven heat, plan preparation in bulk of dishes for freezing by trebling a basic recipe. Cook one portion to serve immediately and two more to freeze down.

Recipes suitable to be treated in this way are marked with the following symbol ✳. They include dishes from throughout this book. Many others besides main-dish casseroles are equally suitable for freezing if properly protected against the cold dry air inside the freezer cabinet.

A casserole with a lid which has a steam vent is perfectly suitable for frozen storage providing you twist a small piece of foil to make a plug for the vent. Dishes without lids should either be topped with a cap of foil smoothed down the sides, or placed in strong polythene bags from which surplus air is extracted before the tie is tightened.

Every food has freezing possibilities

It is fortunate that many fresh foods, such as eggs, which cannot be frozen in the shell, and vegetables with a delicate cell structure, such as cucumber, freeze very well indeed in made-up dishes. For instance, petits pois with sweetcorn (see page 53) includes cooked lettuce leaves; although lettuce cannot be frozen for use in salads.

Pretty desserts which take some time to prepare and present in individual portions can often be made up completely, providing the decoration does not rise above the rim of the container, and covered with cling wrap which only requires to be peeled off when served.

Freezer notes

1. When freezing food with a high water content allow at least one-tenth of the total volume as a headspace so that there is somewhere for the water to expand when it freezes, without damaging the seal. Remember that a shallow wide container with a large surface area may only require a fractional depth as headspace whereas a narrow deep container (such as a sealed tumbler) will require very much more.

2. Casseroles which are not guaranteed to go straight from freezer to oven should be removed from the freezer and at least partially defrosted before being exposed to direct oven heat. It is not necessary fully to defrost the casserole – allow 2–4 hours according to size.

3. Labelling is of vital importance as packs of food soon become anonymous in the freezer. You would not wish to remove the lid from a sealed casserole to identify the contents. Simple colour coding helps, too, when searching for specific items – use green labels for vegetables, yellow for fruit, red for meat, etc.

4. Certain items may be removed from the freezer for use by other members of the family – use large white labels for these and write full instructions for defrosting and cooking. Occasionally you may have prepared too much for a meal and will assemble a simple plate meal covered with foil. The label should state, for example, 'Braised beef, mashed potato, minted peas – Defrost 30 minutes, 30 minutes moderately hot oven'. A foil plate meal can go straight into the oven.

5. Your invaluable casseroles and dishes which can be used for cooking and serving require careful treatment in the freezer. Try to reserve a flat surface in a freezer basket or a special shelf so that they can stand firmly.

6. To save time and partially thawing ice cream so that it can be scooped out, fill small dishes or footed desserts with sufficient scoops to make good portions, cover with cling wrap and place together on a baking sheet or tray in the freezer. Serving is just a question of peeling off the wrap, pouring over a sauce or popping in a wafer.

7. To extract air from a bag either containing some awkwardly shaped item or slipped over a dish, you can use a small vacuum pump. These cost little and are quite efficient. If you do not have one, draw out surplus air with a drinking straw before sealing.

8. For a meal intended to be served only a short time after freezing, it may be practical to freeze down in the casserole used for cooking. For longer-term storage, straight-sided dishes of all shapes and sizes can be lined with foil after cooking and filled with individual or family-sized portions. The food should be partially frozen until it will hold its shape when the foil lining is lifted out. Leave sufficient foil above the top of the dish to fold in and cover the food completely. To serve, strip the foil off the frozen food, and replace in the dish it will fit.

9. A freezerproof plate can be attractively piled up with sandwiches and covered with cling wrap or foil, then stored in the freezer. This saves time as you need only place the plate on the table long enough before the meal for the sandwiches to defrost. Defrosting time is quicker if you remove the covering.

10. To defrost and reheat rolls or scones, they should be unpacked and arranged still frozen on an ovenproof plate. Place immediately in a moderately hot oven for 10–20 minutes, according to the size of the individual items.

Cheesed shepherd's pie *

METRIC/IMPERIAL
1 medium onion, chopped
1 tablespoon oil
350–450 g/12 oz–1 lb roast lamb or roast beef, chopped
150 ml/¼ pint stock
1 teaspoon Worcestershire sauce
3–4 drops gravy browning
salt and pepper to taste
2 large tomatoes, skinned
450 g/1 lb mashed potatoes
when serving :
50 g/2 oz Cheddar cheese, grated
15 g/½ oz butter

AMERICAN
1 medium onion, chopped
1 tablespoon oil
1½–2 cups chopped roast lamb, or roast beef
generous ½ cup stock
1 teaspoon Worcestershire sauce
3–4 drops gravy browning
salt and pepper to taste
2 large tomatoes, skinned
2 cups mashed potato

½ cup grated cheese
1 tablespoon butter

Fry the onion gently in the oil until soft. Add the chopped meat to the onion with the stock, Worcestershire sauce, gravy browning and seasoning to taste. Combine, and place in a medium ovenproof casserole. Slice the tomatoes, and arrange in a layer over the meat mixture. Pipe or fork the mashed potato on top. Cool.

To freeze: Cover with lid, and place in a polythene bag. Seal and label.

To serve: Defrost at room temperature for 4 hours. Uncover, and sprinkle with the grated cheese and dot with the butter. Place in a moderately hot oven (190°C, 375°F, Gas Mark 5) for 45 minutes, until heated through, and golden brown on top.   *Serves 4.*

Lamb with orange slices ✳

METRIC/IMPERIAL	AMERICAN
2 oranges	2 oranges
1 tablespoon cornflour	1 tablespoon cornstarch
300 ml/½ pint stock	1¼ cups broth
50 g/2 oz brown sugar	¼ cup light brown sugar
salt and pepper	salt and pepper
450 g/1 lb cooked leg of lamb, sliced	1 lb cooked leg of lamb, sliced
when serving:	
orange slices	orange slices

Thinly pare the zest (rind) from the oranges and cut into fine shreds. Cook the shreds of zest in boiling water for 10 minutes, then drain. Squeeze the juice from the oranges and combine with the cornflour (cornstarch), shreds of zest, stock and sugar. Season to taste. Place the sliced lamb in a shallow ovenproof dish and pour the sauce over.

To freeze: Cover with lid or foil or put the container inside a polythene bag. Seal and label.

To serve: Defrost for 4 hours at room temperature, then cook in a moderate oven (180°C, 350°F, Gas Mark 4) for 1 hour. Serve garnished with orange slices.   *Serves 4.*

Baked strawberry Alaska ✳

METRIC/IMPERIAL	AMERICAN
4 trifle sponges	12 ladyfingers
4 tablespoons sweet sherry	4 tablespoons sweet sherry
2 tablespoons strawberry jam	2 tablespoons strawberry jam
225 g/8 oz strawberries, sliced	1 cup sliced strawberries
3 egg whites	3 egg whites
175 g/6 oz castor sugar	¾ cup granulated sugar
600 ml/1 pint strawberry ice cream	1¼ pints strawberry ice cream
2 tablespoons flaked almonds	2 tablespoons slivered almonds

Arrange the sponges side by side on an oblong ovenproof platter. Sprinkle over the sherry and spread immediately with jam before the sponges get too soft. Cover with the sliced strawberries. To make the meringue, whisk the egg whites until they form soft peaks. Whisk in half the sugar and continue whisking until the mixture stands in firm glossy peaks. Fold in the remaining sugar. Pile up the ice cream on the sponge and fruit base, leaving a margin of sponge 2·5 cm/1 in wide all round. Quickly swirl the meringue over the ice cream and sponge base and seal it well right down to the platter. Lift up peaks with a round-bladed knife. Sprinkle with almonds.

To freeze: Open freeze until firm then cover lightly with cling wrap. (The meringue never sets hard.)

To serve: Uncover and place the Alaska in the refrigerator cabinet at the beginning of a meal. When required, place in a hot oven (220°C, 425°F, Gas Mark 7) for 4–5 minutes, until the peaks are golden brown, then serve immediately.   *Serves 4.*

A good use for turkey meat is to use it in 'cuts' instead of roasting the bird whole. This is an economical and interesting new method using the family-sized (3 kg/6 lb) frozen turkeys now available from freezer centres. Remove the breasts, skin them and slice into steaks for turkey oriental (for 4). Remove the drumsticks and wings and use the drumsticks and first wing joints for barbecued turkey joints (for 4). Remove the thighs and use to make savoury turkey rolls (for 2). Finally, while you are using the oven, cook the carcase, giblets, neck and the rest of the wings in an ovenproof casserole to make a tasty and sustaining Turkey noodle soup *(for 4–6)*.

Barbecued turkey joints ✱

METRIC/IMPERIAL
*2 raw turkey drumsticks and the first joint
from each of the wings*
50 g/2 oz flour
½ teaspoon salt
¼ teaspoon pepper
¼ teaspoon chilli powder
50 g/2 oz butter, melted
sauce :
2 tablespoons vinegar
75 ml/3 fl oz boiling water
2 teaspoons prepared mustard
25 g/1 oz brown sugar
salt and pepper to taste
pinch of cayenne pepper
2 slices of lemon
25 g/1 oz butter
1 small onion, sliced
3 tablespoons tomato ketchup
2 teaspoons Worcestershire sauce

AMERICAN
*2 raw turkey drumsticks and the first joint
from each of the wings*
½ cup flour
½ teaspoon salt
¼ teaspoon pepper
¼ teaspoon chili powder
¼ cup melted butter

2 tablespoons vinegar
⅓ cup boiling water
2 teaspoons prepared mustard
¼ cup light brown sugar
salt and pepper to taste
dash of cayenne pepper
2 slices of lemon
2 tablespoons butter
1 small onion, sliced
3 tablespoons tomato catsup
2 teaspoons Worcestershire sauce

Remove the skin from the drumsticks and as much skin as possible from the wing joints. Mix the flour with the seasonings and coat the joints well with this mixture. Arrange the coated turkey joints in a greased shallow ovenproof dish and pour over the melted butter. Bake in a moderate oven (180°C, 350°F, Gas Mark 4) for 45 minutes. Mix together all the ingredients for the sauce and place in a small ovenproof casserole. Place in the oven with the turkey joints and cook for 45 minutes. Strain the sauce over the turkey, reduce the oven heat to moderate (170°C, 325°F, Gas Mark 3) and cook for 1–1½ hours, or until the turkey is tender, basting frequently with the sauce. *Serves 4.*

Savoury turkey rolls

Take the 2 turkey thighs and remove the bone from each. Flatten out the pieces of meat, place a ball of ready-made stuffing in the centre of each and roll the meat around it. Wrap each roll in 2 or 3 rashers (slices) of bacon and place in a small ovenproof dish. Bake in a moderately hot oven (200°C, 400°F, Gas Mark 6) for 50 minutes. *Serves 2.*

Turkey noodle soup ✳

METRIC/IMPERIAL	AMERICAN
turkey carcase, giblets, neck and wing tips	*turkey carcase, giblets, neck and wing tips*
1 large onion, sliced	*1 large onion, sliced*
1 large carrot, sliced	*1 large carrot, sliced*
2 celery sticks	*2 celery stalks*
6 peppercorns	*6 peppercorns*
4 cloves	*4 cloves*
1 bouquet garni	*1 bouquet garni*
salt to taste	*salt to taste*
1¾ litre/3 pints boiling water	*7½ cups boiling water*
75 g/3 oz fine noodles	*1 cup fine noodles*
2 tablespoons sherry	*2 tablespoons sherry*

Place the carcase, giblets, neck and wing tips in a large casserole with the vegetables and seasonings. Pour over the boiling water and place in a moderate oven (180°C, 350°F, Gas Mark 4) for 1–2 hours. Strain the stock, cool, then chill it. Remove any pieces of meat from the carcase and wings, and reserve. When the stock is cold, skim off any excess fat. To serve, heat the stock in a saucepan, add the reserved meat and the noodles. Bring to the boil and simmer for about 20 minutes. Check the seasoning and stir in the sherry.   *Serves 4–6.*

Turkey oriental ✳

METRIC/IMPERIAL	AMERICAN
450 g/1 lb raw turkey breast	*4 turkey breast steaks*
salt and pepper to taste	*salt and pepper to taste*
2 tablespoons oil	*2 tablespoons oil*
1 medium onion, chopped	*1 medium onion, chopped*
1 large cooking apple, peeled	*1 large baking apple, peeled*
150 ml/¼ pint water	*generous ½ cup water*
2 teaspoons curry powder	*2 teaspoons curry powder*
1 tablespoon cornflour	*1 tablespoon cornstarch*
375 g/13 oz can pineapple pieces	*13 oz can pineapple pieces*
4 tablespoons cranberry sauce	*4 tablespoons cranberry sauce*
25 g/1 oz flaked almonds	*¼ cup slivered almonds*

Cut 4 100 g/4 oz/¼ lb steaks from the breasts of the turkey, lay them in a greased shallow ovenproof dish and season to taste. Heat the oil and use to fry the onion gently until transparent. Core and thickly slice the apple and add to the onion with the water and curry powder. Bring to the boil and simmer for about 20 minutes, until the apple is very soft. Blend the cornflour with 150 ml/¼ pint/generous ½ cup pineapple syrup, add to the pan and bring back to the boil, stirring constantly. Add the cranberry sauce, stir until it has melted, then pour the sauce over the turkey steaks. Cover with the pineapple pieces and scatter over the almonds. Cover with lid or foil and bake in a moderate oven (180°C, 350°F, Gas Mark 4) for 40 minutes. Serve with oven-baked rice.   *Serves 4.*

Chapter 8
Auto-timed cookery

This kind of cooking makes a lot of dreams come true. The moment at the end of a busy day when you put your key in the lock or ring the front door bell can be depressing. Inside, the table is waiting to be laid and all the messy preparation is still to be done before you can even begin cooking. Hungry people crowd into the kitchen in search of snacks because it is bound to be an hour before the meal is ready.

Instead, you could arrive home from a long day out at work, or for pleasure, to find delicious smells stealing from the kitchen, signalling that dinner is cooked and ready to serve. Perhaps there are last-minute touches to add, or a sauce to make, but the meal is certain to be on the table within minutes of your arrival. The only price to pay for this convenience – quarter of an hour extra spent in the kitchen just before you go out.

If this method of catering becomes a daily custom, you will soon be an expert on creating dinner menus with a difference. The secrets are simple enough. Each dish you choose must fit into a plan, governed by the temperature of the oven and the length of cooking time. You can set the oven low, for a long period, or high for quick cooking, so long as this suits all the food to be cooked. (A sweet to serve cold can be added to the cooking list the day before, bearing in mind the time and temperature it needs.)

Another consideration is that the ingredients must not dry out, curdle or separate while waiting for some hours; and that the recipe works from a cold start.

Most oven cooking assumes putting food into a preheated oven, but sometimes it is just a question of cooking longer, allowing time for the oven to reach the right heat. It is possible to prepare a basic soufflé mixture in the morning, leaving the separated egg whites ready to whisk up when you return home. This is done just before you serve the main course, as many soufflés cook in 25 minutes at high heat. Raise the oven heat as the recipe directs, fold in the stiffly beaten egg whites. Remove all other completely cooked dishes from the oven, and pop it in. A sweet or savoury soufflé often makes a delightful surprise ending to the meal. Do not forget to return the cooker to manual control, or it may switch off after ten minutes, causing total collapse of your soufflé!

Just try an auto-timed supper once at home, and you may easily be converted. Then there is the breakfast problem, if you have guests in the house, and don't wish to appear *en negligée* to get a hasty meal together for them. Or you may just want to sleep late on Sunday when everyone else plans to get up early and go out. Of course advantages like these are greatest of all when you entertain because guests feel less welcome if they can see how much trouble they cause.

There are many occasions when automatic ignition of your oven helps you more than having an extra pair of hands in the kitchen at serving time. So be sure you have as many ovenproof casseroles, shallow dishes, plates, etc., as possible, to help you make good use of this household blessing.

Auto-timed breakfast or brunch for six people

Menu

Cereal in cream
Oeufs en cocotte
Casseroled kippers
French bread in foil
Hot spiced prunes

Work plan

1.   Put 2 tablespoons uncooked quick cook oats in each of 6 buttered oatmeal bowls. Stir 2 teaspoons chopped mixed nuts, ½ teaspoon grated orange zest (rind), 1 tablespoon brown sugar and 100 ml/4 fl oz/½ cup cold milk into each bowl. Cover the dishes with foil and place on the centre shelf of the oven.

2.   Put 2 tablespoons finely chopped ham in the bottom of each of 6 greased ramekins. Break egg carefully into each ramekin, making sure that the yolk remains intact. Gently spoon 1 tablespoon melted butter over each egg and sprinkle with paprika pepper and salt to taste. Put the dishes together on a baking sheet and place on a shelf in the warmest part of the oven.

3.   Spread 12 boneless kipper fillets with soft margarine. Arrange in layers of 4 fillets in a small ovenproof casserole. Cover and place in the oven next to the eggs.

4.   Slice 1 large or 2 small French loaves (Viennas) diagonally almost through to the base at 2·5 cm/1 in intervals. Spread with softened butter on each side of the cuts and wrap closely in foil. Place on a shelf in the coolest part of the oven.

5.   Put 450 g/1 lb tenderized prunes into a small ovenproof casserole. Sprinkle with 1 teaspoon ground cinnamon. Pour over sufficient strained strong, hot tea just to cover the prunes. Cover and place in the oven next to the bread.

6.   Set the oven to moderately hot (190°C, 375F, Gas Mark 5) to switch on 40 minutes before the meal is required. (Before serving check that the eggs will not be overcooked by the time you have eaten the cereal.)

Serving instructions

Uncover the bowls of hot cereal and pour over each a little single cream. Serve with fruit juice if desired. Serve the eggs with the hot bread, followed by the kipper fillets, then the prunes. Make plenty of hot coffee and offer a choice of orange marmalade or fruit preserves to finish up the bread.

Auto-timed lunch for four people

(Illustrated on page 119)

Work plan

1. Peel and slice 4 medium onions. Fry gently in 40 g/1½ oz/3 tablespoons butter until pale golden. Transfer to a medium ovenproof casserole and add 1 crumbled stock (bouillon) cube, 450 ml/¾ pint/2 cups brown ale (beer), 300 ml/½ pint/1¼ cups water, 2 teaspoons mild prepared mustard, and seasoning to taste. Stir well, cover the casserole and place on a shelf in the coolest part of the oven.

2. Fry 4 chicken portions in a further 40 g/1½ oz/3 tablespoons butter until pale golden. Put into a large ovenproof casserole and add 2 sliced onions, 396 g/14 oz can tomatoes, 300 ml/½ pint/1¼ cups red wine, a crushed clove of garlic, 1 tablespoon tomato purée, 4 courgettes (zucchini) cut into chunks, and 1 teaspoon dried mixed herbs. Season with salt and pepper, cover the casserole and place on the centre shelf of the oven.

3. Peel ¾ kg/1½ lb potatoes. Boil until tender, then drain and mash with 25 g/1 oz/ 2 tablespoons butter, 2 egg yolks, and seasoning to taste. Cool and form into 8 balls. Roll the potato balls in chopped almonds. Arrange in a greased shallow ovenproof dish and cover with foil. Place in the oven next to the soup.

4. Peel, core and slice 4 firm pears and place in a shallow ovenproof dish. Add the juice and grated zest (rind) of 1 lemon and 4 tablespoons clear honey. Mix 100 g/4 oz/2 cups soft breadcrumbs with 75 g/3 oz/⅓ cup demerara (light brown) sugar. Place on a shelf in the warmest part of the oven.

5. Set the oven to moderately hot (190°C, 375°F, Gas Mark 5) to switch on 1 hour before the meal is required.

Serving instructions

Toast slices of French bread sprinkled with cheese to serve with the soup. Thicken the juices from the chicken with a little cornflour (cornstarch), if liked. Make up the salad.

Auto-timed lunch for four people

Menu

Casseroled curry soup
Roast chicken with
Roast potatoes and parsnips
Carrots in orange glaze
Cranberry fruit compôte

Work plan

1.   Finely chop 1 large mild onion. Melt 25 g/1 oz/2 tablespoons butter and use to fry the onion until limp. Stir in 1 tablespoon cornflour (cornstarch) and 1 teaspoon curry powder. Cook, stirring, for 3 minutes. Transfer to a medium ovenproof casserole and add 1 crumbled chicken stock cube (bouillon cube). Peel, core and grate 1 large cooking apple and add to the casserole with 1 tablespoon lemon juice and 600 ml/1 pint/2½ cups water. Season with salt and pepper. Cover the casserole and place on a shelf in the coolest part of the oven.

2.   Peel and parboil 4 medium potatoes and 4 medium parsnips. Cut them into halves or quarters as required to make the pieces roughly the same size. Melt sufficient butter to brush over the chicken and coat the potatoes and parsnips. Place the chicken in a shallow ovenproof roasting dish and arrange the vegetables round it. Sprinkle with salt and pepper. Place the dish on a shelf in the centre of the oven.

3.   Peel and slice 4 large carrots. Grate the zest (rind) and squeeze the juice from 1 large orange. Place the sliced carrot in a small ovenproof casserole. Season the orange juice with salt and pepper, and stir in the grated zest. Melt 25 g/1 oz/2 tablespoons butter and add to the orange juice mixture with 1 tablespoon of brown sugar. Pour over the carrots. If necessary, add sufficient water to the dish to just cover the carrots. Cover the casserole and place in the oven next to the chicken.

4.   To make sufficient compôte to have 4 extra servings, cold, place 450 g/1 lb tenderized prunes, 225 g/8 oz/½ lb dried apricots and a 430 g/15 oz can of pineapple chunks in a large ovenproof casserole. Stir in two 175 g/6 oz jars or cans of cranberry sauce. Combine 75 g/3 oz/¼ cup soft (light) brown sugar, 1 tablespoon cornflour (cornstarch) and 4 tablespoons sherry until well blended. Pour over the fruit. Add 600 ml/1 pint/2½ cups water and stir well. Cover the casserole and place in the oven next to the soup.

5.   Set the oven to moderately hot (190°C, 375°F, Gas Mark 5) to switch on 1½ hours before the meal is required.

Serving instructions

Sieve or liquidize the soup, return to the oven to reheat and serve sprinkled with coarsely chopped watercress. Use the juices strained from the glazed carrots combined with those in the roasting dish, sharpened with the addition of 1 tablespoon vinegar, to make a pleasant sweet-sour sauce. Thicken with gravy powder if desired.

   Note : To serve 6 or 8, choose a chicken large enough, increase the quantities of vegetables, and use all the Cranberry fruit compôte if necessary.

Auto-timed dinner for four people

Menu

Mushroom and celery soup
Pork chops with onion and cider sauce
Cheesy potatoes and carrots
Honey baked apples

Work plan

1.   Chop 6 stalks of celery and 1 large onion. Melt 40 g/1½ oz/3 tablespoons butter and use to fry the celery and onion gently until soft. Stir in 4½ teaspoons cornflour and cook for 3 minutes. Transfer to a medium ovenproof casserole and add 1 crumbled chicken stock cube (bouillon cube), 100 g/4 oz/1¼ cups chopped mushrooms, 300 ml/½ pint/1¼ cups water, 300 ml/½ pint/1¼ cups milk, and seasoning to taste. Cover the casserole and place on a shelf in the coolest part of the oven.

2.   Brown 4 pork chops on both sides in 3 tablespoons oil. Put the chops into a large ovenproof casserole. Slice 2 medium onions, add to the fat remaining in the pan and fry gently until soft. Stir in 1 tablespoon cornflour (cornstarch) and cook for 3 minutes. Add 300 ml/½ pint/1¼ cups cider, 150 ml/¼ pint/½ cup water, 1 crumbled stock cube (bouillon cube), and seasoning to taste. Stir well and pour over the chops. Cover the casserole and place on the centre shelf of the oven.

3.   Peel 450 g/1 lb potatoes and 450 g/1 lb large carrots. Slice them both as thinly as possible. Layer the potato and carrot slices in a greased shallow ovenproof dish, dotting each layer with butter and seasoning with salt and pepper. Pour over 150 ml/¼ pint/ ½ cup milk and 150 ml/¼ pint/¾ cup cream. Sprinkle with 75 g/3 oz/¾ cup grated cheese. Put in the oven next to the soup.

4.   Core 4 cooking (baking) apples, place in a shallow ovenproof dish. Fill the centres with raisins and brown sugar and spoon over 4 tablespoons honey and 4 tablespoons water. Sprinkle with ground mixed spice. Place the dish on a shelf in the warmest part of the oven.

5.   Set the oven to moderately hot (190°C, 375°F, Gas Mark 5) to switch on 1 hour before the meal is required.

Serving instructions

Sieve or liquidize the soup, stir in 150 ml/¼ pint/½ cup cream, return to the oven to reheat and serve sprinkled with chopped parsley. Garnish the chops with watercress and serve the apples with custard or cream.

Auto-timed supper for four people

Menu
Hot beetroot soup
Baked cheesy baps
Curried pork pancakes
Orange and watercress salad

Work plan

1.   Peel and grate $\frac{1}{2}$ kg/$1\frac{1}{4}$ lb raw beetroot (beet). Place in a medium ovenproof casserole with scant 1 litre/$1\frac{3}{4}$ pints/$3\frac{3}{4}$ cups strong beef stock (broth) or consommé. Cover and place on a shelf in the warmest part of the oven.

2.   Split 4 large baps (hamburger buns) and spread with soft margarine. Mix together 175 g/6 oz/2 cups grated Gouda cheese and 1 teaspoon prepared mustard with 2 table-spoons salad cream. Divide the mixture among the baps and use to sandwich them together. Place on an oval ovenproof serving dish, cover lightly with foil and place in the oven next to the soup.

3.   Make up a pancake batter with 100 g/4 oz/1 cup plain (all-purpose) flour, 1 egg and 1 egg yolk, 300 ml/$\frac{1}{2}$ pint/$1\frac{1}{4}$ cups milk and 1 tablespoon oil. Use to fry 8 small thin pancakes. Peel, core and grate 1 large cooking (baking) apple, finely slice 225 g/8 oz/$\frac{1}{2}$ lb button mushrooms and finely chop 225 g/8 oz/$\frac{1}{2}$ lb cold roast pork or ham. Combine these with 2 tablespoons sultanas (golden raisins), 2 tablespoons flaked (slivered) almonds and 2 teaspoons curry powder. Fry the mixture gently in 2 tablespoons oil for 5 minutes. Divide the mixture between the 8 pancakes, roll them up and place close together in a shallow ovenproof dish. Drizzle over 2 tablespoons melted butter and place on the centre shelf of the oven.

4.   Set the oven to moderately hot (190°C, 375°F, Gas Mark 5) to switch on 45 minutes before the meal is required.

Serving instructions

Strain the beetroot soup through a fine sieve into 4 warmed individual soup coupes. Stir 1 tablespoon of the cooked beetroot into each coupe and swirl a spoonful of soured cream into each portion of soup. Serve with the cheesy baps. Peel and slice 1 large orange, divide 1 bunch watercress into sprigs, and toss these with 2 tablespoons French (Italian) dressing and the orange slices. Serve with the stuffed pancakes.

An auto-timed lunch for four : onion soup, chicken neapolitaine, with potato and almond croquettes and a green salad. In the foreground, pear streusel.

Chapter 9
Crock pot cookery

In the days when the only methods of cooking were roasting before a fire or gently stewing in a cauldron, the crock pot method was already popular. Food was completely sealed in clay and very slowly baked in the ashes of the fire, or placed in an earthenware or stoneware pot with a strong linen cover tied over it. Then the pot was placed in the cauldron. This, too, usually took all day to cook. Now that we have the modern electric slow cooker, you can enjoy food cooked by the same method to perfection, without trouble.

One feature is invaluable for people who go out to work all day and cannot return to 'watch the pot'. Most dishes cook for up to 8 hours without becoming overcooked. If you come home late the dinner will not have spoiled. It is prepared to wait for you! Regarding nutrition, this method retains vitamins which tend to vanish with quick cooking at a high temperature. There is no loss of moisture so meat becomes tender and stays juicy.

An eye to economy

Now we come to another important factor, that of economy. You can use cheaper cuts of meat and they do not shrink in cooking. The cost of fuel is almost negligible. Because of the crock pot's very low power rating, it uses no more electricity than a light bulb. Suppose you went out and left one light switched on in the house all day, you would not feel you had wasted much electricity. The crock pot uses no more than this to prepare for you a delicious fully cooked meal.

This useful piece of equipment has other advantages too. It is so easy to clean because the gentle cooking process does not bake food on to the inner surface. Although different makes of cooker vary, the casserole itself can often be entirely removed from the electric heating base and washed up like any other pot. It can be taken straight to the table or placed in the oven if you wish.

Bake as well as stew

The crock pot has so many uses that you can even bake or steam puddings in it. For instance, a light fruit cake can be cooked in a greased and floured cake tin inside the slow cooker covered with two or three layers of soft kitchen paper. Sometimes you need to pour hot water round the container in the casserole so that bread or cake is baked by the steaming method. Providing you follow the directions which come with your crock pot, you can cook a great deal more than a simple stew in it.

In fact, its popularity has now extended round the world and good cooks everywhere are creating recipes specially for crock pot cookery.

Two dishes from the crock pot: New Brunswick beef (foreground) and porc à l'Alsacienne.

Useful hints

1.   Menus using the crock pot are more adaptable than you might suppose. Food which takes only 2–3 hours to cook can be prepared in the late afternoon and served for a mid-evening snack for your guests. A dinner party dish which takes 3–4 hours to cook need not be prepared until after lunch. This may mean defrosting items like fish, meat or chicken beforehand. If you are out all day, choose dishes for your evening family meal which take anything between 7 and 10 hours to cook, according to how long the cook expects to be away from home.

2.   Keep the crock pot covered. It should rarely be necessary to remove the lid to stir or check how the food is going. Steam escapes and with it some of your precious heat. It may take as long as 15 minutes to regain the correct cooking temperature so keep peeps and stirs to a minimum and avoid removing the lid during the first 2 hours when baking.

3.   It is a mistake to place frozen foods directly into the slow cooker. They should be thawed beforehand. Defrost items like meat completely; defrost and heat vegetables almost to boiling point. You will notice that recipes usually are worded to take care of this problem.

4.   Many cooks are surprised that because so little evaporation takes place in the slow cooker more liquid is retained than you would find if cooking by other methods.

You will soon learn how to adjust the quantity of seasoning and thickening agent to suit your taste.

5.   If you want to speed up cooking, place a piece of foil on top of the food so that it reflects heat back into it. This is heat which would otherwise be lost through the lid and if your cooker is only capable of very low temperatures this may be a useful tip to know.

6.   Keep and use your crock pot on a flat, level surface where it will be safe from small hands or from being tipped over accidentally. Avoid trailing flex and if there is sufficient length, double up in the middle and secure with a twist tie or elastic band.

7.   If you have no trivet for baking in the crock pot, use an inverted saucer instead.

8.   Always remember that a crock pot with *attached* cord cannot be immersed in water for cleaning. The most satisfactory method is to place the crock in an empty sink, almost fill with warm water and a few drops of detergent, allow to stand for a few minutes, wash round inside carefully and pour out from the side away from the electrical point.

9.   No crock pot should be scratched or scraped on the inner surface to remove traces of cooked food. This practice will eventually form scratches in which food will stick while cooking. If food particles prove stubborn, allow to soak for a longer time.

Corny chicken scrump ✳

METRIC/IMPERIAL
1 clove garlic, crushed
50 g/2 oz flour
1 teaspoon salt
¼ teaspoon black pepper
4 chicken portions
50 g/2 oz butter
pinch of dried oregano
pinch of dried basil
300 ml/½ pint soured cream
150 ml/¼ pint water
1 large green cooking apple
312 g/11 oz can sweetcorn kernels

AMERICAN
1 clove garlic, crushed
½ cup flour
1 teaspoon salt
¼ teaspoon black pepper
4 chicken portions
¼ cup butter
dash of dried oregano
dash of dried basil
1¼ cups soured cream
generous ½ cup water
1 large green baking apple
11 oz can kernel corn

Rub the crock pot well with the garlic then discard. Grease the crock pot then warm it for 20 minutes. Season the flour with the salt and pepper. Use to coat the chicken portions well. Melt the butter and use to fry the chicken portions quickly until golden on all sides. Transfer the chicken to the crock pot, cover and keep hot while making the sauce. Sprinkle remaining flour into the juices left in the pan, together with the herbs. Gradually add the soured cream mixed with the water and bring to the boil, stirring constantly. Season to taste and pour the sauce over the chicken. Cook for about 3–4 hours. Peel, core and thinly slice the apples. Stir in the corn, liquid from the can, and the apple slices, cover and cook for a further 1 hour. *Serves 4.* If frozen, reheat in casserole or saucepan.

New Brunswick beef ✳
(Illustrated on page 120)

METRIC/IMPERIAL	AMERICAN
¾ kg/1½ lb chuck steak	1½ lb chuck steak
50 g/2 oz seasoned flour	½ cup seasoned flour
50 g/2 oz butter	¼ cup butter
3 inner celery sticks with leaves, chopped	3 inner celery stalks with leaves, chopped
1 large carrot, sliced	1 large carrot, sliced
1 medium onion, sliced	1 medium onion, sliced
1 medium parsnip or turnip, diced	1 medium parsnip or turnip, diced
225 g/8 oz can butter beans	8 oz can navy beans
450 ml/¾ pint beef stock	2 cups beef broth
salt and pepper to taste	salt and pepper to taste
3 cloves	3 cloves
2 bay leaves	2 bay leaves

Warm the crock pot for 20 minutes. Trim and cut the meat into 4 thick serving slices. Coat with seasoned flour. Melt the butter in a large saucepan and use to brown the meat slices well on both sides. Transfer to the crock pot. Toss the prepared vegetables in the fat still in the pan. Stir in the rest of the seasoned flour. Add the beans and their liquid, the stock and seasoning to taste. Bring to the boil, stirring constantly and pour over the meat in the slow cooker. Tie the cloves and bay leaves in a piece of muslin (cheesecloth) and place in the centre of the pot. Cook for 6–7 hours, or until the meat is tender. Discard the cloves and bay leaves.   *Serves 4.* If frozen, preheat in casserole or saucepan.

New Zealand lamb and prune casserole ✳

METRIC/IMPERIAL	AMERICAN
¾ kg/1½ lb boneless lamb, cubed	1½ lb boneless lamb, cubed
1 large onion, chopped	1 large onion, chopped
300 ml/½ pint stock	1¼ cups broth
1 teaspoon dried rosemary	1 teaspoon dried rosemary
1 tablespoon sweet mint jelly	1 tablespoon sweet mint jelly
salt and pepper to taste	salt and pepper to taste
1 tablespoon cornflour	1 tablespoon cornstarch
225 g/8 oz tenderized prunes	½ lb tenderized prunes

Warm the crock pot for 20 minutes. Fry the lamb in its own fat with the chopped onion for 5–10 minutes, until the lamb is brown all over and the onion limp. Add the stock, rosemary, mint jelly and seasoning to taste. Moisten the cornflour with a little cold water, add to the pan and bring to the boil, stirring constantly. Transfer to the crock pot and add the prunes. Cook for about 5 hours. Skim off any excess fat and serve immediately with mashed potatoes.   *Serves 4.*

Porc à l'Alsacienne ✳

(Illustrated on page 120)

METRIC/IMPERIAL
100 g/4 oz bacon, chopped
1 large onion, sliced
1 clove of garlic, crushed
¾ kg/1½ lb lean boneless pork, cubed
1 large carrot, sliced
1 tablespoon tomato purée
100 g/4 oz button mushrooms
450 ml/¾ pint white wine or half stock and
  half wine
salt and pepper to taste
1 teaspoon sugar
1 tablespoon cornflour

AMERICAN
¼ lb bacon, chopped
1 large onion, sliced
1 clove of garlic, crushed
1½ lb lean boneless pork, cubed
1 large carrot, sliced
1 tablespoon tomato paste
¼ lb button mushrooms
2 cups white wine or half broth and half
  wine
salt and pepper to taste
1 teaspoon sugar
1 tablespoon cornstarch

Warm the crock pot for 20 minutes. Fry tne bacon, onion and garlic gently together until pale golden. Add the cubed pork and sliced carrot and fry until the meat is brown on all sides. Add the tomato purée, mushrooms, white wine, salt, pepper and sugar and bring to the boil. Transfer to the crock pot and cook for about 6 hours. Moisten the cornflour (cornstarch) with a little cold water. Stir well into the crock pot and cook for a further 30 minutes to 1 hour. Serve garnished with parsley.   *Serves 4.* If frozen, reheat in casserole or saucepan.

Cookery terms

BAKE BLIND – bake pastry by filling un-cooked shell with foil and dried beans and baking in the oven.

BASTE – spoon fat, or sauce, over food during cooking to keep it moist.

BEURRE MANIE – butter and flour kneaded together in the proportion of 3 : 1 then used for thickening sauces and soups. Sauce should be cooked and stirred only long enough to thicken and cook the flour.

COAT – cover food for frying with flour, egg and bread crumbs or with batter.

CREAM – beat fat and sugar with a wooden spoon or mixer until light and fluffy.

DERIND – remove thick skin from bacon or pork.

DESEED – remove core, membranes and seeds from peppers or tomatoes.

DOT – place small pieces of butter evenly over the surface of food such as sliced potatoes before cooking to prevent dry-ing and give a good colour.

DRAIN – remove excess liquid from food.

FLAKE – break cooked fish into pieces with a fork without mashing.

FLUTE – decorate pastry edges with finger and thumb or with a knife before baking.

GRILL – cook food under direct heat in a grill (broiler).

LIQUIDIZE – work food in a blender until it becomes a smooth mixture or liquid.

MARINATE – soak food such as meat in a mixture of oil, acid (wine or vinegar) and seasonings to tenderize it and impart more flavour.

PARBOIL – cook food such as vegetables in liquid until partly cooked. Final cooking to be completed by a different method.

PIPE – press smooth food such as whipped cream through a pastry tube to produce a decorative result.

POACH – cook food such as white fish very gently in liquid to avoid it breaking up.

REDUCE – boil liquid hard to evaporate water and produce a stronger flavour.

RUB IN – cut fat into dry ingredients until the mixture resembles bread crumbs.

SAUTE – fry food briskly in fat in a wide shallow pan until crisp and golden brown.

SIEVE – push food such as raspberries through a strainer to remove skins and seeds.

SIFT – pass dry ingredients such as flour and ground spices through a sifter to remove lumps, mix them uniformly and to introduce air to the food.

SIMMER – cook food in liquid at just below boiling point. Bubbles should rise oc-casionally and break just below the surface.

STEEP – let food stand in hot liquid to extract flavour.

STRAIN – remove all particles of food from a liquid by pouring through a strainer.

TOSS – lift and mix food lightly with two forks until coated with dressing or melted butter.

TRIM – cut away excess fat and skin from meat joints and chops, or remove the roots, leaves, etc. from vegetables.

WEIGHT – press pâtés or terrines with a weight while chilling to produce a firm close texture suitable for cutting.

Index